Music
LANGUAGE
AND
FUNDAMENTALS

MUSIC LANGUAGE AND FUNDAMENTALS

Ronald Gretz
Essex Community College

Wm. C. Brown Publishers

Book Team

Editor *Meredith M. Morgan*
Developmental Editor *Raphael Kadushin*
Production Coordinator *Carla D. Arnold*
Permissions Editor *Mavis M. Oeth*

 Wm. C. Brown Publishers

President *G. Franklin Lewis*
Vice President, Editor-in-Chief *George Wm. Bergquist*
Vice President, Director of Production *Beverly Kolz*
Vice President, National Sales Manager *Bob McLaughlin*
Director of Marketing *Thomas E. Doran*
Marketing Communications Manager *Edward Bartell*
Marketing Manager *Kathleen Nietzke*
Production Editorial Manager *Colleen A. Yonda*
Production Editorial Manager *Julie A. Kennedy*
Publishing Services Manager *Karen J. Slaght*
Manager of Visuals and Design *Faye M. Schilling*

Consulting Editor *Frederick Westphal*

Cover design by Jeanne Marie Regan

The credits section for this book begins on page 249, and is considered an extension of the copyright page.

Library of Congress Catalog Card Number: 88-63888

ISBN 0-697-05359-8

Printed in the United States of America by Wm. C. Brown Publishers, 2460 Kerper Boulevard, Dubuque, IA 52001

10 9 8 7 6 5 4 3 2 1

To my Mother and Father

Contents

Preface

This text is designed for a beginning music education major or a nonmusic major. It explains the various aspects of musical notation in relation to the principles of mathematics and language. Each concept is illustrated by practical musical examples.

The text consists of fourteen chapter with each chapter divided into two parts (a main section and an additional section). The final chapter is a review of all of the material discussed in the text arranged according to the three major elements of music: pitch, rhythm (meter), and harmony.

The main section of each chapter presents *the basic concepts of* music fundamentals. Students will learn to *read* and *identify* musical notation. Some *writing* skills are also incorporated within these sections.

The additional section of each chapter contains sight singing exercises related to concepts discussed in the chapter. (Students should also be encouraged to sing as many musical examples as possible in the main sections of the text.) The additional sections also include keyboard exercises for those instructors who have piano labs, and these exercises again relate to concepts discussed in the chapter. Additional concepts (double accidentals, rhythmic exercises using the half note and eighth note as the pulse note, and so on) appear in the additional sections along with some extra writing exercises.

The additional section of each chapter gives the student a chance to apply the material discussed in each chapter. It gives the instructor the flexibility to adapt this text to individual classes.

While the text examines the *relative* aspects of both rhythm and pitch, it concentrates on examples most frequently used in simple songs. In doing so, the text tries to show *purpose* for each concept it discusses. (For example, various sections attack such questions as why we have different keys, why we need chord inversions, and why we need to be familiar with intervals.)

Finally, the text includes *step-by-step processes to problem solving* along with individual and class exercises. A wide variety of musical examples including classical, pop, broadway, movie themes, hymns, spirituals, folksongs, patriotic songs, and children's songs are used to illustrate the various aspects of music fundamentals.

Acknowledgments

I would like to thank the following reviewers for their comments and criticism which helped tremendously in refining my text: William Kenton Bales, University of Nebraska–Omaha; George Beyer, Cypress College; Robert Cutietta, Kent State University; Arthur S. Danner, West Los Angeles College; Myrna M. Elmore, Portland State University; Marcus Englemann, Allan Hancock College; David J. Ernest, St. Cloud State University; Gayel Gibson, University of Texas–El Paso; Wm. Thomas McKenney, University of Missouri; and Janet Sessions, Phoenix College. A special thanks to Fred Westphal, consulting editor of Wm. C. Brown Publishers, for his valuable comments during the development of this text. And finally a personal thanks to Raphael Kadushin, developmental editor, for his advice and guidance through the process.

Chapter **1** *The Notation of Pitch*

As children we **hear** and learn to **speak** the English language. As we become educated we are taught to **read** and **write** it. We have all **heard** music. Some of us have even learned to **speak** it by singing or playing a musical instrument. Yet few of us have learned to **read** and **write** music.

The following musical example may seem to you as impossible to read as Chinese or Greek, yet you hear this nonverbal language almost every day of your life (sometimes consciously, through concerts, records, compact discs, and so on; and sometimes unconsciously, through the background music on television, in movies or in an office or store).

In the following chapters, we will study symbols and elements of the language of music. Through this study you will learn to read and better understand this universal language.

The Musical Alphabet

The musical language has an alphabet of only seven letters:

A   B   C   D   E   F   G

It will be beneficial for you to know the musical alphabet backwards:

G   F   E   D   C   B   A

Sound

Sound can be classified into two types: regular vibrations (pitch) and random vibrations (noise). The study of music concentrates mainly on pitch. Noise, however, can be used very effectively in music—for example, through percussion instruments of indefinite pitch. This notation is basically rhythmic (as will be discussed in chapter 2).

A sound is audible to the human ear if its *frequency* is between 16 and 20,000 vibrations per second. (The frequency of the notes produced by a piano varies between 30 and 3,000 vibrations per second.)

Frequency can be defined as the number of vibrations per second produced by a vibrating body. Pythagoras, the Greek scholar of the sixth century B.C., discovered that a string stretched between two supports produced a certain pitch when plucked. If the string were stopped midway, the pitch would become twice as high.

For example, if a string vibrates at 440 vibrations per second, the same string, when halved, would vibrate at 880 vibrations per second. Consequently, the *higher* the pitch the *shorter* the string, and the *lower* the pitch the *longer* the string. (Compare the sound and size of a violin string to that of a double bass string.)

The Staff

The seven letters of the musical alphabet represent seven different pitches or musical sounds. These pitches are placed on a staff (plural = staves), which originated as one line separating high and low pitches.

High

Low

Later, the staff was increased to four lines

and at one point in music history, it had as many as eleven lines:

Today the staff consists of five parallel lines that support all musical notation. The staff shows only the *relationship of pitch* (high or low).

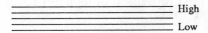

The lines and spaces of a staff are usually numbered from bottom to top:

Lines   Spaces

Any line or space on the staff can represent *any* pitch (A, B, C, D, E, F, or G).

Clefs

A clef (from the French word meaning "key used to unlock") is place on the staff to identify the letter name of the pitch. The names of the lines and spaces depend upon which clef is used. Three different clefs have evolved from the letters they identify: G, F, and C. We will limit our discussion to only two clefs (G and F). [See Additional Exercises at the end of the chapter for a brief explanation of the C clef.]

The G Clef

This is the symbol used for the G clef or treble (high) clef. This clef is used to locate pitches of high frequencies.

When placed on the staff, the treble clef circles the second line, marking it as G.

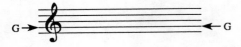

Exercise 1

Copy the treble clef symbol until you can write it from memory. (The following diagram shows a simplified way to write the treble clef symbol.)

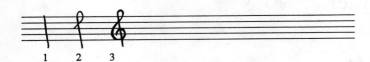

By marking the second line as G, the treble clef also identifies all other lines and spaces.

If a letter is on a **line,** when it repeats it will be on a **space,** and vice versa. Do not make the mistake of thinking that all Gs are on lines and all As are on spaces.

Octaves

An octave (eight) is the distance in pitch between a note and the next repetition of its letter name. For example:

Ledger (Leger) Lines

A ledger line is an extension of the staff above or below the usual five lines. For example:

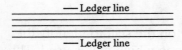

Ledger lines are equidistant from the staff and long enough for only one note.

Use only as many ledger lines as are necessary to notate the desired pitch.

Reading Pitches in the Treble Clef

Study the following pitches.

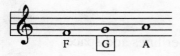

The notes surrounding G are F and A.

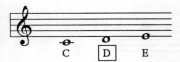

The notes surrounding D are C and E.
The note C is written on a ledger line.

Exercise 2

Name each of the following pitches. (In each example, one of the pitches is G or D.)

Study the following pitches.

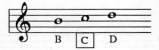

The notes surrounding C are B and D.

The notes surrounding F are E and G.

Exercise 3

Name each of the following pitches. (In each example, one of the pitches is C or F.)

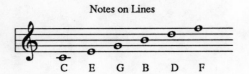

Exercise 4

Name each of the following pitches.

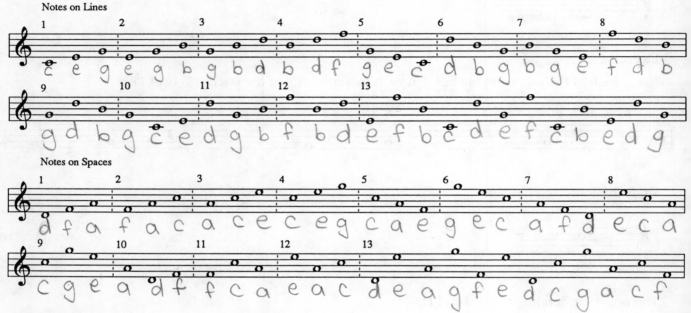

Exercise 5

Name each of the following pitches in the treble clef.
For class participation:

A. The instructor names the first pitch, then a student names the next two pitches.
B. Each student names a set of three pitches.

Now let's relate the treble clef to reading music.

Exercise 6

The following examples show the pitches of songs using notes in the treble clef. Name the pitches. (Write letter names below each pitch.)

Old Folks at Home (Way down upon the Swanee River) (S. Foster)

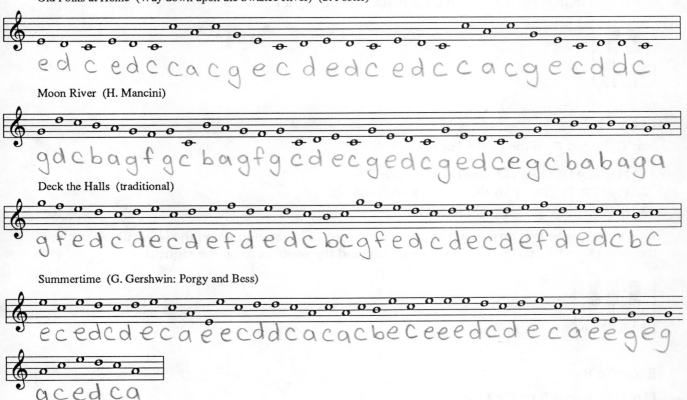

e d c e d c c a c g e c d e d c e d c c a c g e c d d c

Moon River (H. Mancini)

g d c b a g f g c b a g f g c d e c g e d c g e d c e g c b a b a g a

Deck the Halls (traditional)

g f e d c d e c d e f d e d c b c g f e d c d e c d e f d e d c b c

Summertime (G. Gershwin: Porgy and Bess)

e c e d c d e c a e e c d d c a c a c b e c e e e d c d e c a e e g e g

a c e d c a

The Piano Keyboard

The piano keyboard consists of fifty-two white and thirty-six black keys (for a total of eighty-eight). The black keys are arranged in alternating groups of twos and threes, with the exception of the lowest black note on the piano. (This single note is actually the third note of a group of three.)

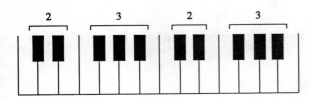

It is beneficial to learn the keyboard for several reasons:

1. It helps one visualize pitches and their relationships.
2. It is easy to produce a given sound on a keyboard. (It is difficult to produce accurate pitches on some instruments—brass, woodwinds, strings—without regular practice.)
3. Keyboard instruments are capable of sounding many pitches simultaneously. (Although this is possible on other instruments it is usually extremely difficult. One exception is the guitar.)
4. Because of the wide range of the keyboard, one can apply knowledge of both the G and F clefs. (Some instruments only require knowledge of one clef.)
5. Beginning students should be able to perform the fundamentals of music discussed in this book on the piano (or other keyboard instrument) with only a little practice.

Pitch Location

The grouping of the black notes helps us identify the white notes. (We will study the identification of black notes in chapter 4.)

On the piano find any group of *two* black notes. The white note on the left will *always* be C, the white note in the center D, and the white note on the right E.

Exercise 7

Play C, D, and E on the piano. For example:

1. Play any D. Then play the D one octave lower.
2. Play any E. Then play the E two octaves higher.
3. Identify more Cs, Ds, and Es on you own.

On the piano find **any** group of *three* black notes. The white note on the **left** will *always* be F, the next two white notes G and A respectively, and the white note on the **right** B.

Exercise 8

Play F, G, A, and B on the piano.
For example:

1. Play any G, then play any G below or above.
2. Play every F on the piano.
3. Identify more Fs, Gs, As, and Bs on your own.

Drawing the Keyboard

Since you may not always have a keyboard to look at, let's learn to draw it quickly. [The following example is one octave from C to C.]

1. Draw nine vertical lines and connect them across the bottom.

2. Draw boxes halfway down on lines 2, 3, 5, 6, and 7.

3. Fill in these boxes.

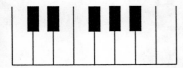

4. Identify the notes.

Exercise 9

In the following space, draw the keyboard from C to C and identify the white notes. Follow the four steps just outlined. Repeat this exercise, drawing the keyboard from memory.

The Location of Notes in the Treble Clef

The **clef** is used to show the *specific* location of a pitch on the keyboard. High pitches on the piano are located on the **right,** low pitches on the **left.** Since the treble clef locates pitches of high frequencies, notes in the treble clef are usually played on the keyboard with the right hand.

On the wood directly above the keyboard you should see the name of the maker of the piano (Steinway, Baldwin, Yamaha, and so on). On the keyboard directly under the name you will see a group of two black notes. The white note to the left is called middle C and is written below the staff on a ledger line in the treble clef. If is the fourth C from the lowest note on the piano.

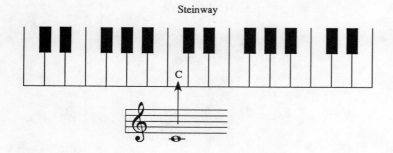

The specific location of all of the notes previously studied in the treble clef is as follows:

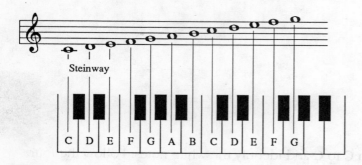

Exercise 10

Notate on the staff the exact pitch shown on each keyboard.

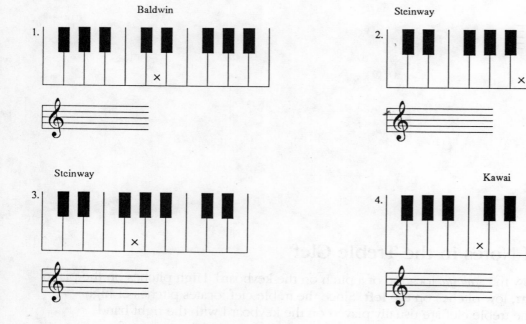

Exercise 11

Place an **X** on each keyboard to show the exact placement of the note on the staff.

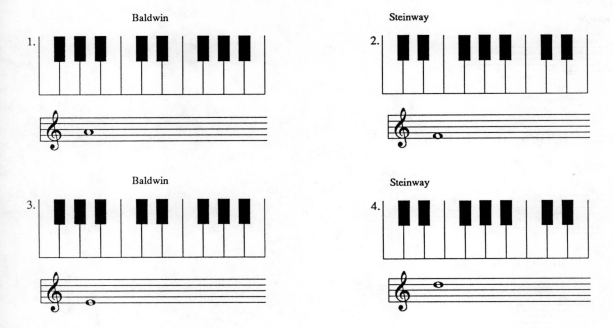

The F Clef

A second clef, 𝄢 the F clef or bass (Low) clef is used to locate pitches of low frequencies.

When this clef is placed on the staff, the two DOTS of the clef should fall above and below the fourth line, marking it as F.

Exercise 12

Copy the bass clef symbol on the staff. The symbol starts immediately below the fourth line, curves up to the fifth line and then swings down to the first line. Place the two dots on spaces three and four.

By marking the fourth line as F, the bass clef identifies all the other lines and spaces.

Ledger Lines in the Bass Clef

Ledger lines are used in the bass clef in exactly the same way as they are in the treble clef. For example:

B   C   D   E   E   D   C

Reading Pitches in the Bass Clef

Study the following pitches.

E   F   G

The notes surrounding F are E and G.

A   B   C

The notes surrounding B are A and C.
The note C is written on a ledger line.

Exercise 13

Name each of the following pitches. (In each example, one of the pitches is F or B.)

F G   B A   B C   F E   G F   C B   E F A   B

Study the following pitches.

B   C   D

The notes surrounding C are B and D.

F   G   A

The notes surrounding G are F and A.

Exercise 14

Name each of the following pitches. (In each example, one of the pitches is C or G.)

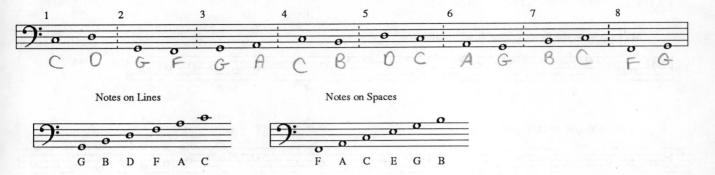

Exercise 15

Name each of the following pitches.

Exercise 16

Name each of the following pitches in the bass clef. For class participation:

A. The instructor names the first pitch, then a student names the next two pitches.
B. Each student names a set of three pitches.

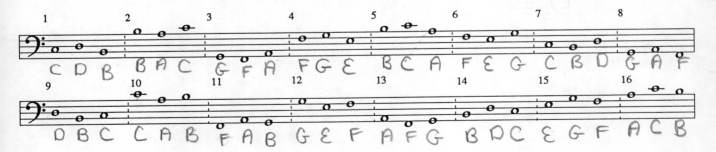

Exercise 17

The following examples show the pitches of songs using notes in the bass clef. Name the pitches. (Write the letter names below each note.)

Michael, Row the Boat Ashore (traditional)

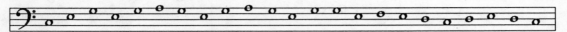

Yankee Doodle (traditional)

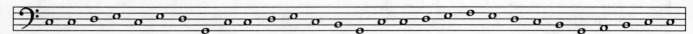

Home on the Range (D. Kelley and B. Higley)

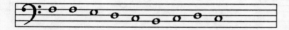

Shenandoah (traditional)

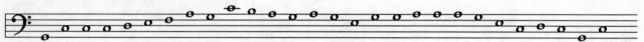

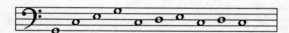

Since the bass clef locates pitches of low frequencies, notes in the bass clef are usually played on the keyboard with the left hand. **Middle C** is written above the staff in the bass clef.

Steinway

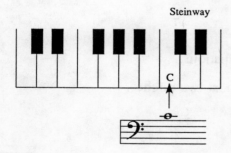

The specific location in the bass clef of all of the notes previously studied is as follows:

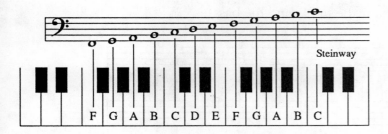

Exercise 18

Notate on the staff the exact pitch shown on each keyboard.

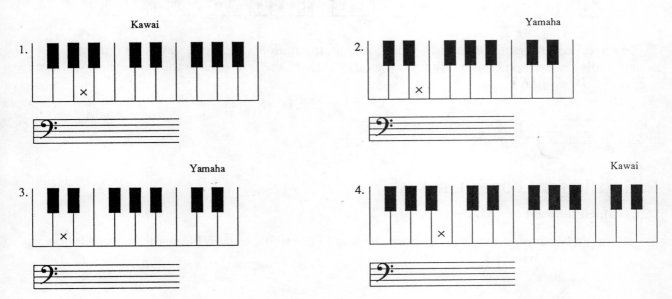

Exercise 19

Place an **X** on each keyboard to show the exact placement of the note on the staff.

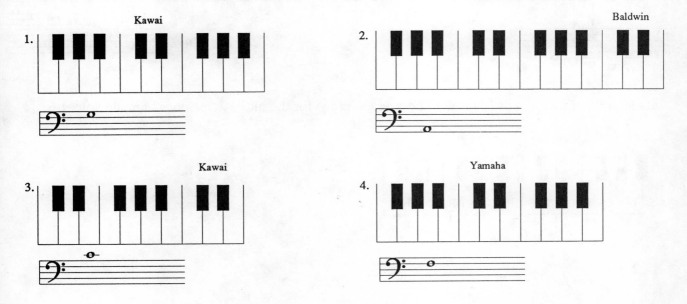

The Grand Staff

The grand staff is actually two staves combined (the treble and the bass).

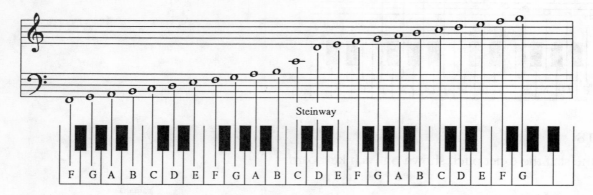

In the preceding example, middle C is written in the middle of the two staves. In musical notation this C is written equidistant from the other lines of the staff (below the treble clef or above the bass clef), as shown:

Rationale for Ledger Lines

Ledger lines are used to

1. Write pitches higher than the G above the staff in the treble clef and lower than the F below the staff in the bass clef.

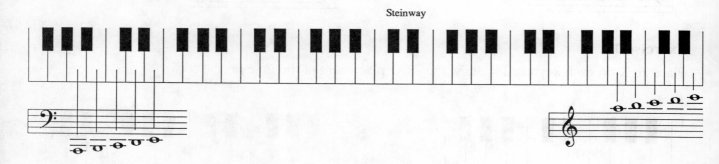

2. Simplify notation. For example: The average range for the alto voice (lowest female voice) is:

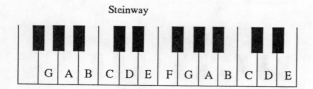

Chapter 1

All of these pitches are written in the treble clef except three:

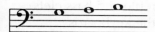

Thus, it seems logical to notate these three notes in the treble clef so that the singer only has to read one clef.

Compare the following two examples of notation:

Extremely difficult notation

Simple, clear notation due to ledger lines

Exercise 20

Identify the following pitches.

Exercise 21

Write the following pitches above or below the staff as indicated. (Not all answers require ledger lines.)

Exercise 22

The following examples include the pitches of songs using notes in both the treble and bass clefs (including ledger lines). Write the names of the pitches below each note. On the keyboards provided, identify the *lowest* and *highest* pitches for each song.

Example:

Battle Hymn of the Republic (traditional melody)

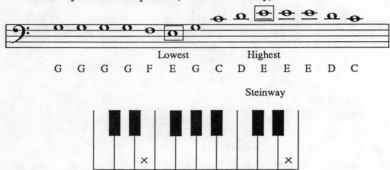

Somewhere Over the Rainbow (H. Arlen: The Wizard of Oz)

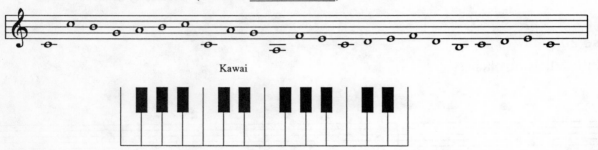

Auld Lang Syne (Should auld acquaintance be forgot) (traditional melody)

Joy to the World (G. F. Handel)

When the Saints Go Marchin' In (spiritual)

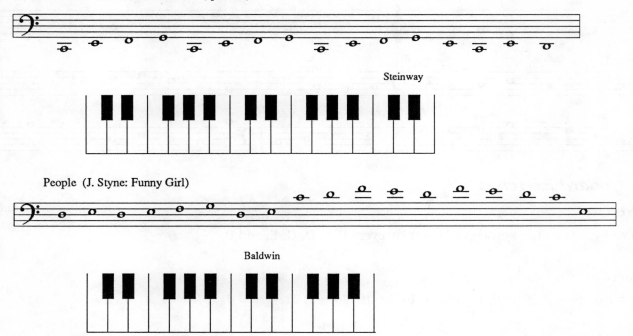

Steinway

People (J. Styne: Funny Girl)

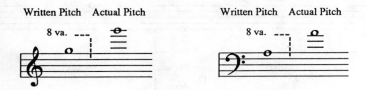

Baldwin

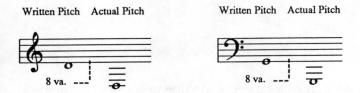

8 va.

To avoid too many ledger lines, the following notation is sometimes used: 8va. = Octave. Dotted lines above the note indicate that the pitch will sound an octave higher.

Dotted lines below the note indicate that the pitch will sound an octave lower.

Additional Exercises

Sight Singing Exercises

Exercise 1

Sing the following sets of pitches. Use the vowel "ah."

Keyboard Exercises

Exercise 1

Play every C on the keyboard. Then play every F, A, D, G, E, and B.

Exercise 2

Play exercises 2, 3, 5, 10, 11, 13, 14, 16, 18, 19, 20, and 21.

Exercise 3

Play the following pitches, first without observing the 8va. marking, then playing the pitch an octave higher or lower as indicated.

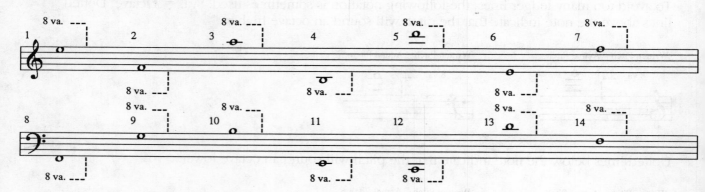

Other Exercises

C Clefs

A third clef is used to locate middle C. The curves in the clef meet at the line designated as middle C. There are four C clefs. The first two listed here are the most frequently used.

Alto (or Viola) clef locates middle C on the third line

Tenor clef locates middle C on the fourth line

Soprano clef locates middle C on the first line

Exercise 1

Say the letter names of the following pitches—first all the pitches in the treble clef, then all the pitches in the bass clef.

Repeat the exercise, naming four notes in the treble clef, then four notes in the bass clef (follow the groups in this order: bar 1, then bar 4; bar 2, then bar 5; bar 3, then bar 6, and so on).

For class participation: Have each student name a set of four pitches. The instructor should randomly choose any of the twelve groups of pitches below.

Exercise 2

Make the following pitches the given letter name by adding a treble or bass clef. For example:

The third space is E in the bass clef.

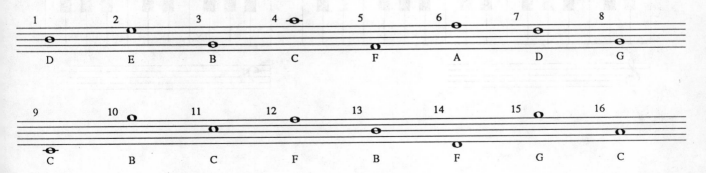

Exercise 3

Write the following notes on lines or spaces as indicated. (If a letter is on a **line,** the octave above or below will be on a **space.**)

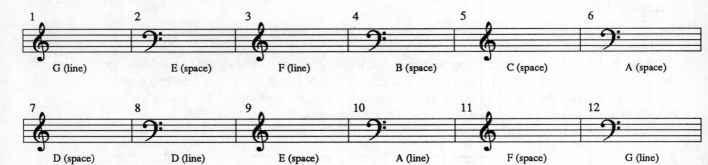

1	2	3	4	5	6
G (line)	E (space)	F (line)	B (space)	C (space)	A (space)

7	8	9	10	11	12
D (space)	D (line)	E (space)	A (line)	F (space)	G (line)

Exercise 4

Notate on the staff the exact pitch shown on each keyboard. (Play each example on the piano.)

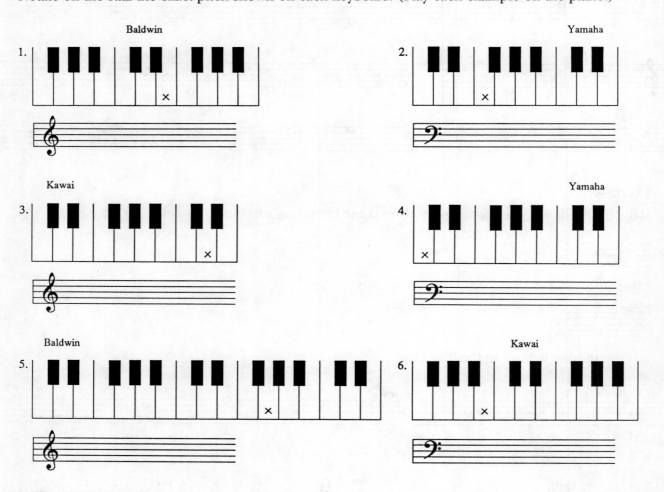

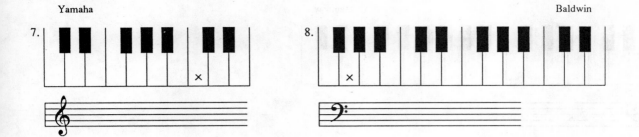

Exercise 5

Place an **X** on each keyboard to show the exact placement of the note on the staff. (Play each example on the piano.)

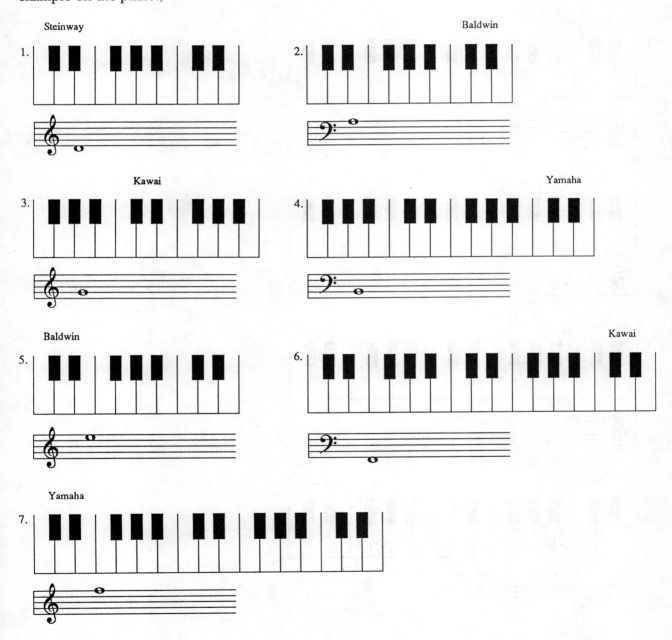

8.

Steinway

Exercise 6

Notate on the staff the exact pitch shown on each keyboard. Some of the examples require ledger lines. (Play each example on the piano.)

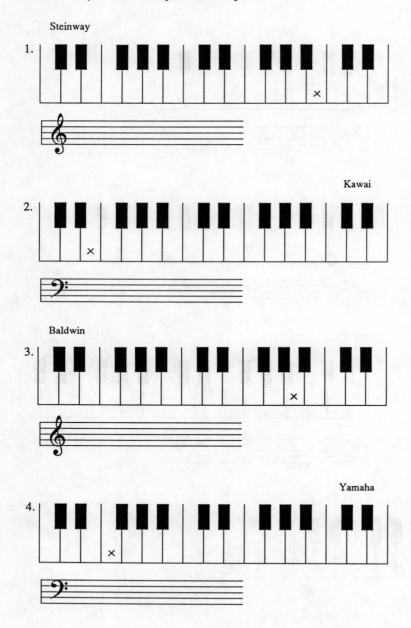

Steinway

1.

Kawai

2.

Baldwin

3.

Yamaha

4.

Exercise 7

Place an **X** on each keyboard to show the exact placement of the note on the staff. Some of the examples use ledger lines. (Play each example on the piano.)

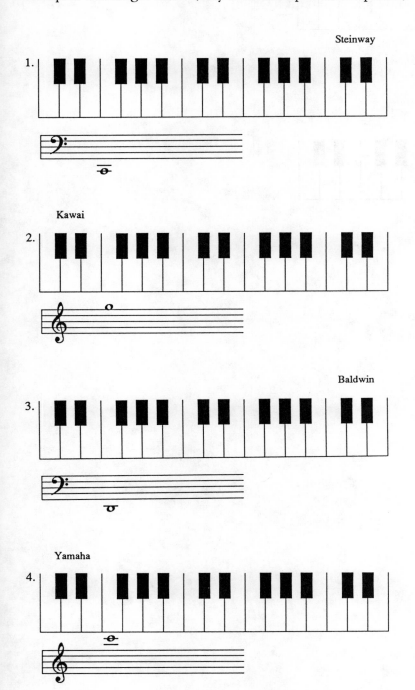

Notation of Pitch

25

5.

Kawai

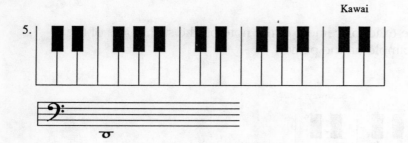

Baldwin

6.

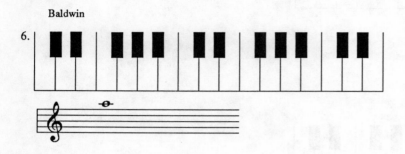

Chapter 2 *The Notation of Rhythm*

If we reexamine the song "Do Re Mi" (see the first muscial example in chapter 1), we will discover that we can now **read** all the pitches. The notes in the melody are easy to read, while those in the piano accompaniment would take more time to identify because of the great number of ledger lines. For the moment, let's concentrate only on the first seven notes of the melody.

Although at first glance these notes seem similar, they actually show many varied characteristics of musical notation.

The first six notes are filled in, while the seventh is not. All seven have lines (stems) extending upwards, two (the first and third) have dots, and two (the second and fourth) have curved lines to the right of the stem (flags).

The purpose of these different characteristics of notes is to identify the duration of each sound. This aspect of music, referred to as **rhythm,** is based on simple mathematics.

There are six ways to change the duration of pitch. First let's consider the following three:

1 | 2 ●   3 ♭ ♪

Stem   Fill in   Flag added to a Stem

Parts of Notes

Stem → ♭ ← Head / ← Flag

Types of Notes

o Whole Note

♩ Half Note (The addition of a stem **halves** the value of a whole note.)

♩ Quarter Note (Filling in the head of a half note **halves** its value.)

♪ Eighth Note (The addition of a flag to a stem **halves** the value of a quarter note.)

♬ Sixteenth Note (Each additional flag **halves** the value of the preceeding note.)

These changes in notation must proceed in the following order: (1) Add a stem, (2) fill in the note head, and (3) add one or more flags.

It is incorrect in our notation system to take a whole note (o) and change its value by just filling it in (●). Filled-in notes *must* have stems. Similarly, it is incorrect to add a flag to a half note (β). Flags can only be added to notes that are filled in.

Stems and Flags

Stems are added **upward** on the **right** side of the note head and **downward** on the **left**.

Flags always go to the **right**.

Exercise 1

Change each of the whole notes to half notes by adding stems. (Alternate the direction of the stems—first up, then down.)

Change each of the whole notes to quarter notes by first adding a stem, and then filling in the head of the note. (Alternate the direction of the stems.)

Change each of the whole notes to eighth notes by first adding a stem, then filling in the head of the note and finally adding a flag. (Alternate the direction of the stems.)

Change each of the whole notes to sixteenth notes by first adding a stem, then filling in the head of the note and finally adding two flags. (Alternate the direction of the stems.)

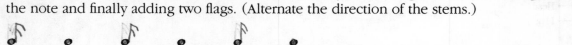

Remember, each additional flag **halves** the value of the preceeding note (β thirty-second note, sixty-fourth note). These notes are less common in our system.

Placing Notes on the Staff

When placed on the staff, the head of the note is placed on a line or space to make the desired pitch. For example:

General Rules for Adding Stems

When the note head is **above the middle line of the staff** (regardless of the clef) the note stem points **downward.** For example:

When the note head is **below the middle line of the staff** (regardless of the clef) the note stem points **upward.** For example:

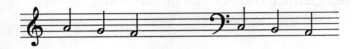

When the note head is **on the middle line** (regardless of the clef) the note stem may point **up or down.** For example:

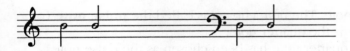

Exercise 2

Place a stem on each of the notes in the following songs according to the general rules just discussed.

Exercise 3

Write the following types of notes on the staff, making each the desired pitch. Place note stems according to the general rule. (All notes in this exercise will not require a stem).

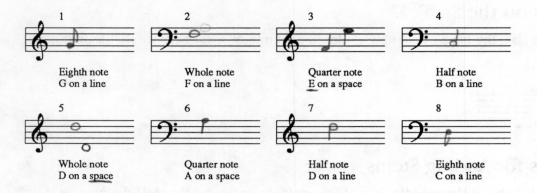

1	2	3	4
Eighth note G on a line	Whole note F on a line	Quarter note E on a space	Half note B on a line
5	6	7	8
Whole note D on a space	Quarter note A on a space	Half note D on a line	Eighth note C on a line

We now know the relative values of notes. (A quarter note is half as long as a half note and twice as long as an eighth note.) Next let's give these notes a specific rhythmic (numerical) value.

Let's return to our musical example, "Do Re Me."

Immediately after the treble clef sign is a **time signature** (meter signature) consisting of two numbers. The *bottom* number identifies the type of note that counts as one beat.

Beat

A **beat** is a constant pulsation. It acts as a ruler by which we can measure the length of sound. The length of a beat is expressed mathematically as "one." (If you tap your foot four times at a constant pulse, you have performed four beats.)

The beat can be represented by any type of note. The note chosen is called the **pulse note** (or beat note). The most frequently used pulse note is the quarter note.

In the song "Do Re Mi" we can tell that the quarter note has been chosen as the pulse note because the bottom number is 4 (signifying one quarter).

If: the quarter note receives one beat   ♩ = 1

Then: the eighth note receives one-half beat   ♪ = 1/2

the half note receives two beats   ♩ = 2

the whole note receives four beats   o = 4

The *top* number in the time signature identifies the **meter.**

Meter

When a constant pulse is grouped into *regular* stresses or accents it is called a **meter.** The two basic meters are **duple** and **triple.**

Duple (2) | |

     Accented/Unaccented (one strong beat followed by one weak beat)

Triple (3) | | |

     Accented/Unaccented/Unaccented (one strong beat followed by two weak beats)

One of the most frequently used meters is **quadruple** (a grouping of four). Quadruple is actually a duple meter repeated.

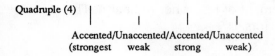

Quadruple (4)

Accented/Unaccented/Accented/Unaccented
(strongest   weak   strong   weak)

Since the first beat is always the strongest, we can consider quadruple meter as an accented beat followed by three unaccented beats.

The song "Do Re Mi" is in a duple meter because the top number in the time signature is 2. (See the example at the beginning of the chapter.)

Bar Lines

To show that we have come to the end of a grouping of beats, we insert a vertical line called a bar line. The distance between two bar lines is called a **measure** or **bar.**

Bar line →   Measure (Bar)   ← Bar line

Any arrangement of notes can make a measure as long as every measure contains *exactly* the number of pulse notes expressed in the time signature. For example, in quadruple time, one measure might contain a single whole note (four counts). Another might contain three quarter notes (three beats) plus two eighth notes (one beat) for a total of four counts.

Double Bars

A double bar is used to show the end of a section of music or the end of the piece. The second bar line is double the thickness of the first.

Exercise 4

Identify the meter (duple, triple, or quadruple) of the following songs.

1. Sing the song.
2. Tap a constant pulse.
3. Group the beats into regular stresses.

Example: Jingle Bells

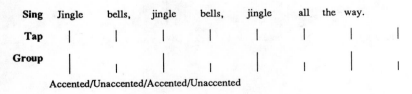

| Sing | Jingle | bells, | jingle | bells, | jingle | all | the | way. |

Tap

Group

Accented/Unaccented/Accented/Unaccented

"Jingle Bells" is written in a duple meter.

Somewhere Over the Rainbow   triple   Alouette   quadruple

Yankee Doodle   quadruple   Silent Night   triple

Conducting Patterns

One of the many responsibilities of a conductor is to establish and keep a constant beat. Instead of tapping a foot, the conductor conveys the beat with the movement of his or her right arm. The following are standard patterns of movements used by conductors.

Duple Meter

Down—Up (Conductor pauses slightly at the lowest and uppermost points in the pattern)

Triple Meter

Down—To the right—Up

Quadruple Meter

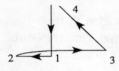

Down—To the left—Across—Up

Exercise 5

Instructor: Ask a member of the class to conduct one of the following songs while the rest of the class sings a cappella (unaccompanied).

Conducting patterns correspond to the **top** number of the time signature. Each of the following examples begins on the **first** beat.

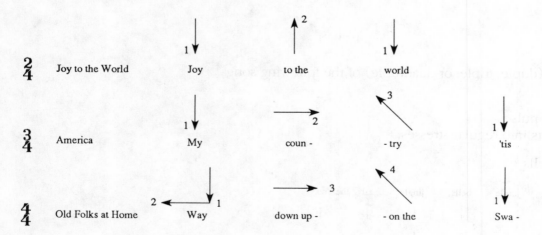

Simple Meters

Any meter which has a time signature in which the top number is 2, 3, or 4 is called a simple meter. These numbers tell the grouping of the beat (both accented and unaccented). In simple meters the bottom number of the time signature represents the type of note chosen as the pulse note, or the type of note that is counted as one beat. Bottom numbers are usually 4 (quarter note) but may also be 2 (half note) or 8 (eighth note). The numbers 1 (whole note) and 16 (sixteenth note) are possible but rarely used.

The symbol **C** is used as a substitute for $\frac{4}{4}$ time and is usually referred to as "common time" since it is the most frequently used time signature. The symbol **¢** is used as a substitute for $\frac{2}{2}$ time and is usually referred to as "cut time" or "alla breve." In this meter the half note is the pulse note and the meter (grouping) is duple (accent, no accent).

Exercise 6

Divide the class into two groups and perform the following rhythms.

Everyone taps the beat.
Group One counts the beats aloud (duple meter: 1, 2; triple meter 1, 2, 3; quadruple meter 1, 2, 3, 4)
Group Two sings the rhythm (using "ta"; pronounced tah)
For example:

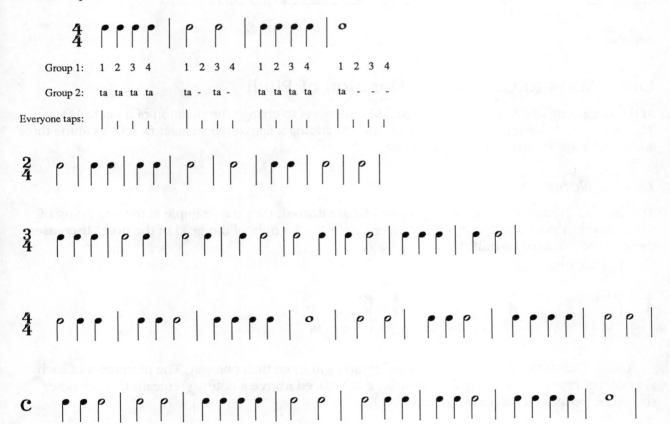

Exercise 7

In each of the following songs identify the meter (duple, triple, quadruple) and the pulse note.

America (My Country, 'tis of Thee) (traditional)

Meter:
Pulse Note:

Jacob's Ladder (traditional)

Meter:
Pulse Note:

Yankee Doodle (traditional)

Meter:
Pulse Note:

Alouette (French folksong)

Meter:
Pulse Note:

Other Ways to Change the Duration of Pitch

At the beginning of this chapter we discussed three ways to change the duration of a pitch: (1) adding a stem, (2) filling in the note head, and (3) adding a flag to the stem. Now let's examine three additional ways to change the duration of a pitch.

Dotted Notes

The first and third notes of the song "Do Re Mi" are **dotted.** (See the example at the beginning of the chapter). A dot placed immediately **after** a note (to the right of the head of the note) **increases** the value of that note by **half.**

For example:

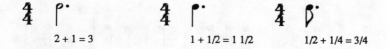

$$2 + 1 = 3 \qquad 1 + 1/2 = 1\ 1/2 \qquad 1/2 + 1/4 = 3/4$$

(Note: Our notational system uses some symbols in more than one way. The placement of each symbol has a specific meaning. For example, a dot placed **above** a note • means that the note should be performed **staccato,** or detached.)

Exercise 8

Identify the meter and pulse note for each of the following songs. Write the rhythmic value (number of beats) below each note then draw bar lines to show the end of each measure.

Example:

America

Rhythmic values: 1   1   1   1 1/2   1/2   1   1   1   1   1 1/2   1/2   1   1   1   1   3
Meter: Triple simple
Pulse note:

Bar lines added to the song:

Deck the Halls (traditional)

Rhythmic values:
Meter:
Pulse Note:

Moon River (H. Mancini)

Rhythmic values: 3   1   2   1½   ½   ½   ½   2   1   1½   ½   ½   ½   2   1   3
Meter:
Pulse Note:

My Funny Valentine (R. Rodgers: Babes in Arms)

Rhythmic values:
Meter:
Pulse Note:

Tied Notes

In measures seven and eight of "Do Re Mi" the note F is **tied.**

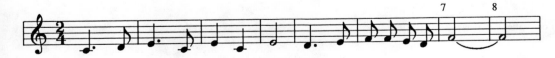

Notes of the same pitch joined by a tie (⌒ or ‿) are connected rhythmically, forming one length. The value of the second note is added to that of the first. (The tie in music is similar to the + sign in mathematics.)

Notes are tied together for several reasons:

1. To form lengths that cannot be expressed by a single note

2 + 1/4

2. To connect notes from one measure to another

This is the case in "Do Re Mi". The pitch F is to be held for four beats; however, there can only be two beats in a measure of $\frac{2}{4}$ time. Thus, two half notes are tied together in consecutive measures to indicate that the note is held for four beats.

It is also possible to tie more than two notes of the same pitch. For example:

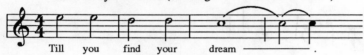

Climb Ev'ry Mountain (R. Rodgers: The Sound of Music)

Till   you   find   your   dream ————— .

Notes are always tied from note head to note head.

Correct   Incorrect

Exercise 9

Write the values of the tied notes below each tie in the following songs.
Example:

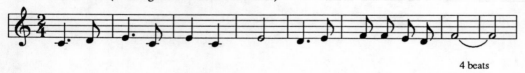

Do Re Mi (R. Rodgers: The Sound of Music)

4 beats

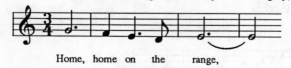

Home on the Range (D. Kelley and B. Higley)

Home, home on   the   range,

Goodnight, Ladies (E. Christy)

Good-night, la-dies —————— good-night, la-dies —————— good-night, la-dies,——— we're going to leave you now.

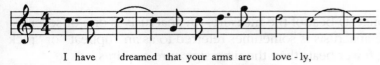

I Have Dreamed (R. Rodgers: The King and I)

I have dreamed that your arms are love - ly,

The Ballad of John and Yoko (J. Lennon and Y. Ono)

Stand - ing in the dock of South - amp - ton,

People (J. Styne: Funny Girl)

Peo - ple, peo - ple who need peo - ple,

A **slur** connects notes of different pitch. In vocal music, a slur indicates that a word or syllable is held through two or more pitches. *The slur has nothing to do with rhythm.*

Example:

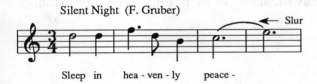

Silent Night (F. Gruber)

← Slur

Sleep in hea - ven - ly peace -

Fermata

There are times when a composer does not want to assign an *exact* number of beats to a sound. In such cases the length of the note changes with each performance. The musical symbol used in such a case is called a **fermata** ⌢ . (The word *fermata* comes from the Italian word *fermare,* meaning "to stop." *Fermata* means to stop the beat that is measuring the length of the sound.)

The song "Happy Birthday" contains a fermata. Tap a beat and sing the song. What word in the song is written with a fermata?

In the song "On the Street Where You Live" from the musical *My Fair Lady,* the first two notes are both written with a fermata and should be held longer than their written values.

On the Street Where You Live (F. Loewe: My Fair Lady)

I have of - ten walked down this street be - fore

Exercise 10

Find a song that includes a fermata. Bring it to class and discuss why you think the composer used a fermata at that particular place in the song.

Two other aspects of rhythm can be found in the song "On the Street Where You Live": the anacrusis, and rests.

The Anacrusis

Many pieces do not begin on the first (strongest) beat of the measure. An anacrusis is one or several notes that occur **before** the first pulse. The anacrusis is sometimes referred to as an "upbeat" or "pick up." It is an "incomplete" measure, having fewer beats than the time signature requires.

In the song "On the Street Where You Live," the first two notes are the anacrusis. Following are two other examples of the anacrusis.

Simple Gifts (Shaker song)

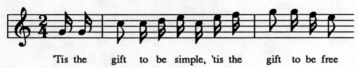

'Tis the   gift   to be simple, 'tis the   gift   to be free

Home on the Range (D. Kelley and B. Higley)

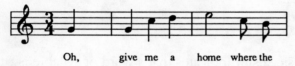

Oh,   give me   a   home where the

Exercise 11

Which of the following songs have an anacrusis? Identify the meter of each song. Write the rhythmic value (number of beats) for each note.
Example:

The Star Spangled Banner (traditional melody)

Rhythmic values: 3/4   1/4   1   1   1   2
               Oh ———— say can you   see

The "Star Spangled Banner" is written in triple simple meter and has an anacrusis.

Somewhere Over the Rainbow (H. Arlen: The Wizard of Oz)

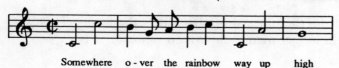

Somewhere o - ver the rainbow   way up   high

Hey,   Jude,   don't make it   bad,

Were You There? (spiritual)

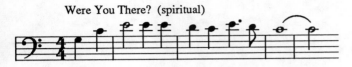

Were you there when they cru-ci-fied my Lord?

Yankee Doodle (traditional)

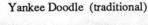

Yankee   Doodle   came to   Lon-don

When a piece begins with an anacrusis, the last measure of the song should contain only a sufficient number of beats to make a complete measure when added to the anacrusis.

America the Beautiful (S. Ward)

Oh,   beau-ti-ful for spa-cious skies   from   sea to shining   sea.

1 beat   3 beats

Rests

In the song "On the Street Where You Live" there is a quarter note **rest** (𝄽) in the second measure. A rest is a symbol for the duration of **silence.** The notation is a simple one—for every note value there is a corresponding rest symbol.

Note Value   Corresponding Rest

𝅝   𝄻

𝅗𝅥   𝄼

𝅘𝅥   𝄽

𝅘𝅥𝅮   𝄾

Any note with a flag has a corresponding rest with the same number of flags. For example:

3 Flags   3 Flags

Rests, like notes, may be dotted:

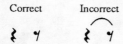

Rests are **never** tied.

Correct   Incorrect

When placed on the staff, the whole rest **hangs** from the fourth line (regardless of the clef).

The half rest **sits** on the third line (regardless of the clef).

All other rests are usually placed in the center of the staff.

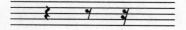

Exercise 12

Write each rest four times on the staves below.

Whole   Half

Quarter   Eighth

Some composers and editors indicate a complete measure rest in $\frac{3}{4}$ time with a whole rest ▬ . For example:

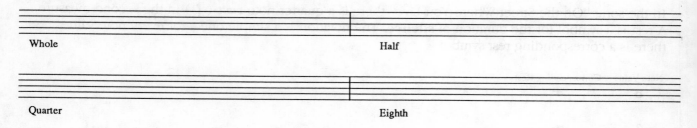

My Favorite Things (R. Rodgers: The Sound of Music)

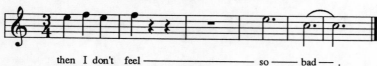

then I don't feel ———————— so —— bad —— .

Exercise 13

The following songs have incomplete measures (marked with an X). Complete the measures, using rests. (Some examples may require more than one rest.)
Example:

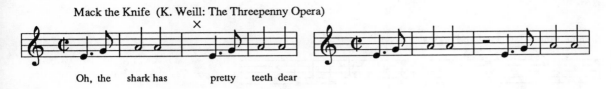

Mack the Knife (K. Weill: The Threepenny Opera)

Oh, the   shark has   pretty   teeth dear

Do Re Mi (R. Rodgers: The Sound of Music)

Do   re mi   fa so la ti   do

Joy to the World (H. Axton)

Je - re - mi - ah was a bull - frog,   was a good friend of   mine.

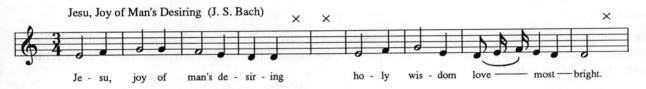

Jesu, Joy of Man's Desiring (J. S. Bach)

Je - su,   joy of   man's de - sir - ing   ho - ly wis - dom love —— most —bright.

We now have the ability to read the rhythm of songs in simple meters. Let's combine this knowledge with our ability to read pitches (chapter 1).

Exercise 14

Make a complete musical analysis of the following songs. Identify all pitches. Identify the time signature (meter and pulse note). Determine the rhythmic value (number of beats) for every note. Circle all rests and record their rhythmic values. Do any of the songs contained an anacrusis or fermata?

1.   Shenandoah (traditional)

Oh,   Shen - an - doah,   I long to   hear you,

I Want to Hold Your Hand (J. Lennon and P. McCartney)

Oh, yeah,   I'll   tell you   some - thing,   I

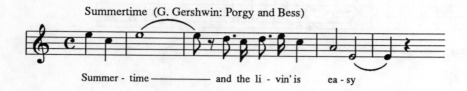

Summertime (G. Gershwin: Porgy and Bess)

Summer - time ———— and the li - vin' is   ea - sy

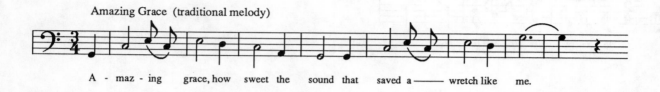

Amazing Grace (traditional melody)

A - maz - ing   grace, how   sweet   the   sound   that   saved a ——— wretch like   me.

Additional Exercises

Sight Singing Exercises

Exercise 1

For each of the following examples, tap a beat and sing only the rhythm. Then sing only the pitches (*without* rhythm). Finally, sing each example with the correct pitches and rhythm. (Sing letter names of the notes or an "ah" vowel.)

Keyboard Exercises

Exercise 1

Play each exercise *slowly:* first play the right hand part (treble clef), then the left (bass clef). Repeat each exercise three times. The purpose of this exercise is to develop the independence of each finger. Before beginning each exercise, place your hand over the five pitches. (The number **1** represents the **thumb** and **5** the **little finger.** This is the same for both hands.)

After you are comfortable playing all of the exercises, try playing both hands together.

Other Exercises

Exercise 1

Write the following rhythmic values (number of beats) using either dotted or tied notes. (It is essential to identify the meter and pulse note **before** you assign a rhythmic value to any note.)

Problem   Solution

4/4   **4/4**
5 beats

2/4   **4/4**   **3/4**
4 beats   2 1/2 beats   5 beats

¢   **C**
1 1/2 beats   3 beats

Chapter 3 *Rhythmic Patterns*

Let's return to the song "Do Re Mi." In measure 6, observe how the four eighth notes in the melody are written separately, however, in the accompaniment these notes are connected (**beamed**).

In vocal music, notes are generally *not* connected. Each note is written separately, corresponding to a syllable of the text. In Instrumental music, however, notes *are* usually beamed together.

Adding Beams to Notes

A beam is simply a horizontal flag. Consequently, only notes with flags can be beamed. (Never beam whole, half, or quarter notes.) The eighth note is the largest note that can be beamed.

Beams, or horizontal flags, are not connected haphazardly but are joined for clarity. Beaming should help make the meter clear by showing where beats begin and end.

Notes are beamed together to:

1. Make a pulse note

Notes of different values may be beamed together to form the pulse note.

2. To make a division of the pulse note

$$\frac{2}{4} \quad ♩. \quad ♪♪ \quad = \quad ♩. \quad \sqcup$$

In this example, the two sixteenth notes are beamed together because their value is equal to an eighth note (a division or fraction of the pulse).

Rhythmic Patterns

Whenever notes are beamed together they form patterns. Music, like language, should be read in patterns, not individual units (that is, we read words and not letters). Learning a few basic rhythmic patterns will prove very helpful in reading music.

Patterns Using the Quarter Note as the Pulse Note

If the quarter note is the pulse note, possible time signatures are: $\frac{2}{4}$ $\frac{3}{4}$ $\frac{4}{4}$ C

Patterns:

1 ♩   Pulse Note

   1   (Suggested syllables)

2 ♫   Division of the Pulse Note

   1 and   (Suggested syllables)

3 ♬   Subdivision of the Pulse Note

   1 ee and uh   (Suggested syllables)
   (1 ee an-duh)

Exercise 1

Tap or clap a beat. Sing one measure in a $\frac{4}{4}$ meter using pattern 1 (the pulse note).

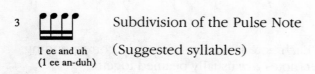

Pattern 1   ♩   ♩   ♩   ♩

Sing: 1   2   3   4   (Suggested syllables)

Tap or clap: | | | |

Tap or clap a beat. Sing one measure in a $\frac{4}{4}$ meter using Pattern 2 (the division of the pulse).

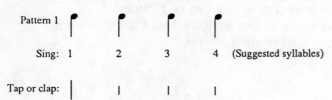

Pattern 2   ♫   ♫   ♫   ♫

Sing: 1   and   2   and   3   and   4   and   (Suggested syllables)

Tap or clap: | | | |

Tap or clap a beat. Sing one measure in a 𝟒/𝟒 meter using Pattern 3 (the subdivision of the pulse).

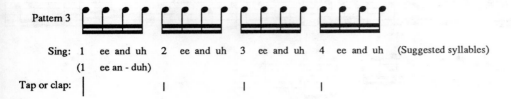

Pattern 3

Sing: 1   ee and uh   2   ee and uh   3   ee and uh   4   ee and uh   (Suggested syllables)
       (1   ee an - duh)

Tap or clap:

Exercise 2

The following songs contain the three patterns just discussed in addition to notes that are longer than the pulse note. Sing the rhythms (using the suggested syllables), visualizing the patterns. Tap or clap the beat. (If the pulse note is dotted, change it to a tied note. This will make the pattern clear.)
Example:

Alouette (French folksong)

Patterns: 1   2   1   1   2   2   1   1
Sing: 1   and 3   4   1 and   2 and 3   4

Each example may also be used as a note reading exercise. Just read the letter names of each pitch in rhythm.

Yankee Doodle (traditional)

Sabbath Prayer (J. Bock: Fiddler on the Roof)

Around the World in Eighty Days (V. Young)

Già il sole dal Gange (A. Scarlatti)

When I Was A Lad (Gilbert and Sullivan: H.M.S. Pinafore)
(Chorus)

Patterns:

4   Long, short, short

    1   and uh   (Suggested syllables)

5   Short, short, long

    1 ee and   (Suggested syllables)

6   (Dotted pattern) Long, short

    1   uh   (Suggested syllables)

Exercise 3

For individual students: Tap or clap a beat. Sing one measure in a **4/4** meter using Pattern 4. (Repeat, using Patterns 5 and 6.)

For class participation: Divide the class into two groups. *Group One:* Tap or clap a beat. *Group Two:* Tap or clap the subdivision of the beat (Pattern 3).

Everyone: Sing one measure in a **4/4** meter using Pattern 4. Repeat, using Patterns 5 and 6. Alternate groups.

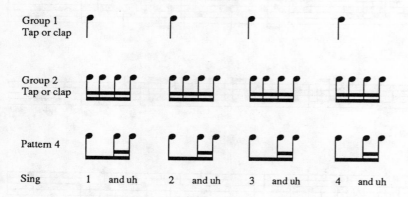

Group 1
Tap or clap

Group 2
Tap or clap

Pattern 4

Sing   1   and uh   2   and uh   3   and uh   4   and uh

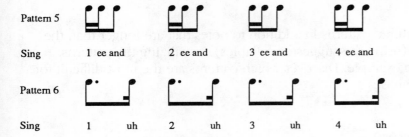

Pattern 5				
Sing	1 ee and	2 ee and	3 ee and	4 ee and
Pattern 6				
Sing	1 uh	2 uh	3 uh	4 uh

Exercise 4

For individual students: Tap or clap a beat. Sing one measure of each Pattern (1–6) in a **4/4** meter.

For class participation: Divide the class into two groups as in exercise 3. Sing one measure of each Pattern (1–6) in a **4/4** meter. Alternate groups.

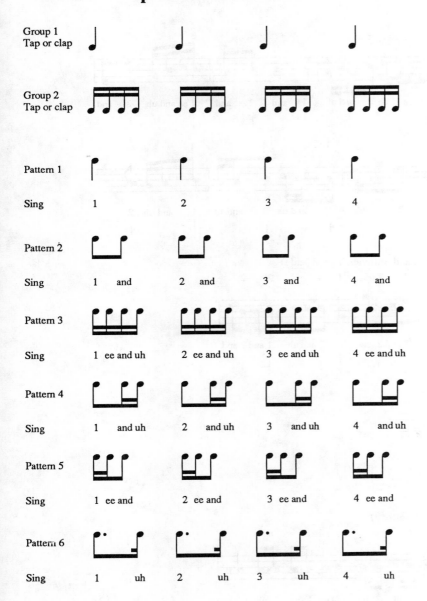

Group 1 Tap or clap				
Group 2 Tap or clap				
Pattern 1				
Sing	1	2	3	4
Pattern 2				
Sing	1 and	2 and	3 and	4 and
Pattern 3				
Sing	1 ee and uh	2 ee and uh	3 ee and uh	4 ee and uh
Pattern 4				
Sing	1 and uh	2 and uh	3 and uh	4 and uh
Pattern 5				
Sing	1 ee and	2 ee and	3 ee and	4 ee and
Pattern 6				
Sing	1 uh	2 uh	3 uh	4 uh

Exercise 5

The following pieces contain all six rhythmic patterns in addition to notes that are longer than the pulse note. Tap a beat. Sing the rhythm (using the suggested syllables), visualizing the patterns. (Pattern numbers are written above each example. Discover which patterns are the most difficult for you and review them in the previous exercises.)
Example:

Visualizing Patterns with Rests

In chapter 2, we learned that rests are symbols notating the duration of silence. (Review the symbols for rests.) When performing pieces with rests, **vocalize** the rest the first time through (sing the complete pattern), then repeat the piece, **observing** the rest.

If You Want to Know Who We Are (Gilbert and Sullivan: <u>The Mikado</u>)

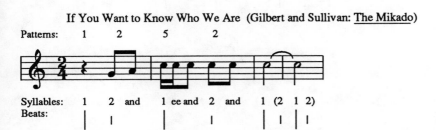

Visualizing Patterns when Notes Are Tied

In performing music with ties, visualize the patterns rather than the number of beats a tied note is held.

Piano Sonata in C Major (k. 309) 3rd. Movement (W. A. Mozart)

Rather than thinking that the first note receives one and one-quarter beats, visualize the two

patterns ♩ ♫♫ . Sing both patterns without the tie, then repeat, observing the tie.

Exercise 6

The following pieces contain rests and/or ties. Tap a beat. Sing the rhythm (using the suggested syllables). Pattern numbers are written above each example. If you have problems with a particular pattern, review that pattern (exercise 4).

3.   I Want to Hold Your Hand (J. Lennon and P. McCartney)

Patterns: 2   6   1 1   2   6 1   2   2   1 1   1   6   1 1   2   6   1

Syllables: 4 and   1 uh 2   (3)   4 and   1 uh 2   (3 4)   (1) and 2 and 3 4   1   (2 3)   4   1 uh   2   (3)   4 and   1 uh   2   (3 4)

Patterns: 2   2   1   2   2   2   1 1   6   6   5   1   2   2   1 1   1

Syllables: (1) and 2 and 3   4   and   (1 2 3 4)   (1) and 2 and 3   4   1 uh 2 uh 3 ee and (4)   (1) and 2 and 3   4   1 (2) (3)

                Summertime (G. Gershwin: Porgy and Bess)

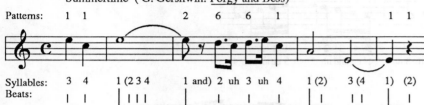

Patterns: 1   1   2   6   6   1   1   1

Syllables: 3   4   1 (2 3 4   1 and) 2 uh 3 uh 4   1 (2)   3 (4   1)   (2)

Additional Exercises

Sight Singing Exercises

Exercise 1

Tap a beat and sing only the rhythm. Then sing only the pitches *without* rhythm. Finally, sing the example with both pitch and rhythm. (Sing either the letter names of the pitches or an "ah" vowel.)

Keyboard Exercises

Exercise 1

Play the following exercises as follows: first with the right hand, then the left hand. Count the rhythm aloud as you play. The purpose of this exercise is to combine pitch and rhythm reading and to continue developing independent finger movements. After you are comfortable playing each hand separately, try playing both hands together.

Other Concepts and Exercises

Using the Half Note and Eighth Note as The Pulse Note

In chapter 2, we learned that *any* note may be the pulse note. The quarter note is the most frequently used pulse note; however, many pieces use the eighth note or half note as the pulse note.

Exercise 1

Tap a beat and sing patterns 1, 2, and 3 using the quarter note as the pulse note.
Patterns

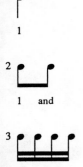

1
1

2
1   and

3
1 ee and uh

Without changing the *speed* of the beat, sing the following patterns, using the half note and the eighth note as pulse notes. (The suggested syllables remain the same.)

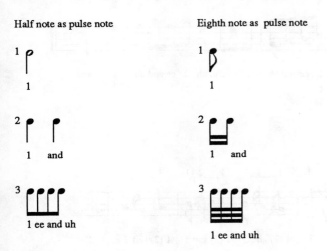

Half note as pulse note

1
1

2
1   and

3
1 ee and uh

Eighth note as pulse note

1
1

2
1   and

3
1 ee and uh

In each case these rhythmic patterns *sound* exactly the same because they have the same *relationship* to the pulse note. (Do not be confused by flags. The elimination or addition of a flag does *not* change the pattern. In mathematics, ½, ²⁄₄, ⁴⁄₈, and ⁸⁄₁₆ all describe the same relationship. Higher numbers *do not* indicate a larger relationship.)

Exercise 2

The following pieces contain these three patterns using the half note and the eighth note as the pulse note. Tap a beat. Sing the rhythm (using the suggested syllables), visualizing the patterns. (Pattern numbers appear above each example.)

1.   Lasst Uns Erfreuen (Geistliche Kirchengesänge, Cologne 1623)

2. There is a Balm in Gilead (spiritual)

(Observe in this song that notes are *not* beamed together just because they have flags. Since the eighth note is the pulse note, notes are beamed together to equal the eighth note.)

3.   Piano Sonata k. 284 (W. A. Mozart) (orig. in D)

4. We Gather Together (Netherlands folksong)

(Again, observe the way the notes are beamed.)

Like the first three patterns, patterns 4, 5, and 6 *sound* the same but have a different *look* when they use a different pulse note.

Tap a beat and sing patterns 4, 5, and 6 using the quarter note as the pulse note.

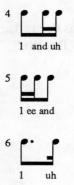

Without changing the speed of the beat, sing the following patterns using the half note and the eighth note as pulse notes. (The suggested syllables remain the same.)

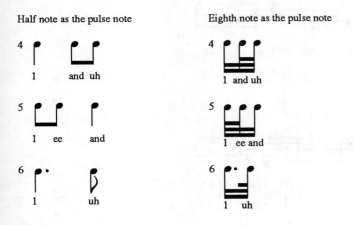

Exercise 3

The following songs contain all six patterns using the half note and the eighth note as the pulse note. Tap a beat. Sing the rhythm (using the suggested syllables), visualizing the patterns. (Pattern numbers appear above each example.) The last two examples contain rests and ties.

4.   My Funny Valentine (R. Rodgers: <u>Babes in Arms</u>)

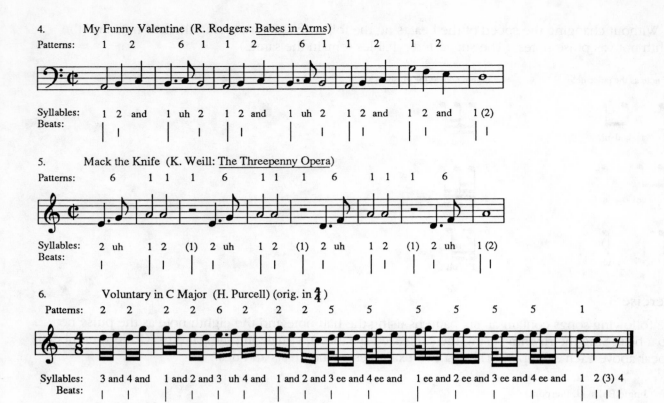

5.   Mack the Knife (K. Weill: <u>The Threepenny Opera</u>)

6.   Voluntary in C Major (H. Purcell) (orig. in 4/4)

Chapter **4** *Accidentals*

Let's return to the song "Do Re Mi"

Tea, a   drink with jam and bread;   that will bring us back to doe!

In measures 25–28 of the melody you'll see two new symbols:

> ♯ in measure 26 (in front of the first two notes—F and G)
>
> ♭ in measure 28 (in front of the last note—B)
>
> These symbols are called **accidentals.**

Before discussing accidentals, let's review the piano keyboard. The piano is divided into twelve equal semitones (or half-steps). On the piano a half-step is the distance between any two adjacent notes.

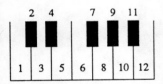

For example, a half-step is the distance between numbers 1 and 2 (white key 1 to black key 2, black key 2 to white note 3, and so on).

Accidentals are used to identify the black keys on the keyboard. However, the word *accidental* is *not synonymous* with *black key.*

Any note on the piano is **higher** in pitch than the notes to its left. (Recall from chapter 1 that the pitch of a musical sound is determined by its frequency.) For example, the pitch of black key (4 in the preceding diagram) is higher than the pitch of notes 1, 2, or 3.

Accidentals

Accidentals are signs that **raise** a pitch, **lower** a pitch, or **restore a pitch to its unaltered state.**
Three symbols are used to signify accidentals in our notational system.

Symbol	Name	Purpose
1. ♯	Sharp	Raises a pitch one half-step

On the keyboard a sharp is the adjacent note to the **right.**
For example:

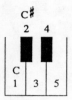

The pitch of C♯ (key 2) is one half-step **higher** than the pitch C (key 1).

2. ♭	Flat	Lowers a pitch one half-step

On the keyboard a flat is the adjacent note to the **left.**
For example:

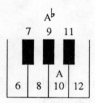

The pitch of A♭ (key 9) is one half-step **lower** than the pitch A (key 10).

3. ♮	Natural	Cancels a sharp or flat

A natural restores a note to its unaltered state.
For example:

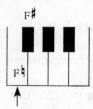 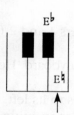

On the keyboard a natural is **always** a white note. (See Chapter 1, Identification of White Notes on the Keyboard.)

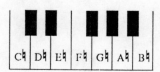

Exercise 1

Identify the following black keys by placing a ♯ or ♭ symbol after the letter name of the pitch, marked on the white key.
For example:

Identification of black key: D♯   G♭

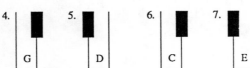

Although naturals are always white notes, flats and sharps are *not always* black notes. There are two places on the keyboard with adjacent white notes (E, F and B, C).

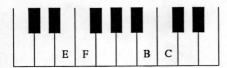

Since the adjacent note to the right of E is the white note F, F can also be called E♯.

Similarly, since the adjacent note to the right of B is the white note C, C can also be called B♯.

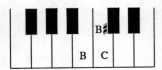

The adjacent note to the left of C is the white note B. Therefore, B can also be called C♭.

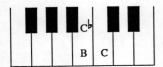

The adjacent note to the left of F is the white note E. Therefore, E can also be called F♭.

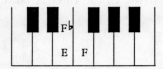

Accidentals on the Staff

Accidentals are placed *before* a note *on the same line or space as the note head.*

Examples:

This note is written as "sharp C," but is read as "C Sharp."

This note is written as "flat G," but is read as "G Flat."

Exercise 2

Name the following pitches (including the accidentals).
Example:

G sharp

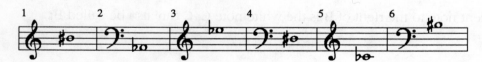

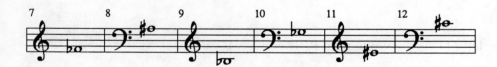

Enharmonic Notes

We just learned that since E and F are adjacent white notes, F can also be called E♯. On the piano, F and E♯ **sound** the **same.** This means that they are **enharmonic** (they share the same pitch but have different letter names).

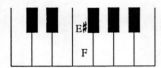

In the English language there are many words that *sound* the same but have different spellings and, consequently, different meanings. For example:

to (preposition)   I went **to** the store.

too (adverb)   It was **too** warm to wear a sweater.

two (adjective)   I bought **two** compact discs.

Pitches must be "spelled" correctly according to their meanings. We'll discuss these meanings in the sections on chromatic and diatonic half-steps (later in this chapter), scales (chapter 5 and 7), intervals (chapter 9), chords (chapter 10).

Enharmonic Spelling

Every black note has two spellings. For example, the black note between C and D can be identified as C♯ or D♭.

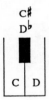

Exercise 3

Enharmonically spell the following black notes.

1. F | G   2. D | E   3. A | B   4. G | A

Each white note may have several spellings; we need only concern ourselves with two examples:

F♭ E♯ | E F   C♭ B♯ | B C

Exercise 4

Enharmonically write the following pitches, then locate each on the given keyboard. For example:

Steinway

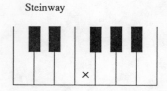

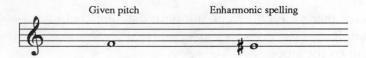

Given pitch   Enharmonic spelling

Steinway

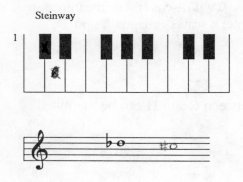

1

Yamaha

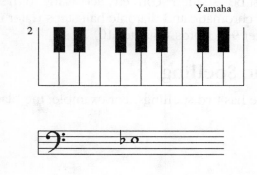

2

Baldwin

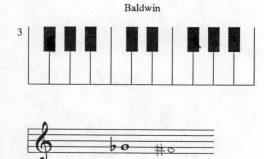

3

Kawai

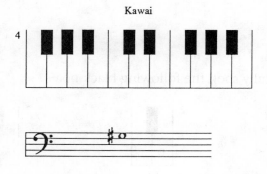

4

Steinway

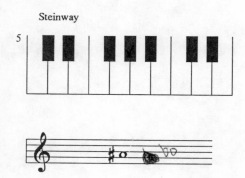

5

Yamaha

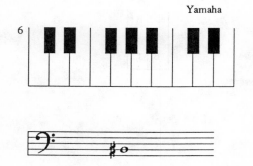

6

Chromatic and Diatonic Half-Steps

The word *chromatic* is a musical term referring to the adjustment of a letter name by the use of an accidental. Therefore, a chromatic half-step must be spelled using the *same letter name*. For example:

G up a chromatic half-step is G♯.

G down a chromatic half-step is G♭.

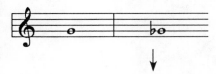

The word *diatonic* is a musical term referring to *adjacent* letter names. Therefore, a diatonic half-step must be spelled using a *different letter name*. For example:

G up is a diatonic half-step is A♭.

G down a diatonic half-step is F♯.

There are two cases when the diatonic half-step does *not* require an accidental: between B and C and between E and F.

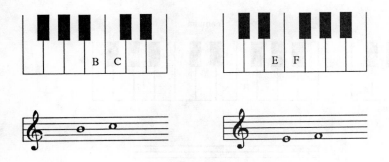

Exercise 5

On the following keyboards you'll see an X placed to the right or left of a designated pitch. On the staff provided, write the designated pitch and the correct **diatonic** spelling of the note marked with an X.

Example:

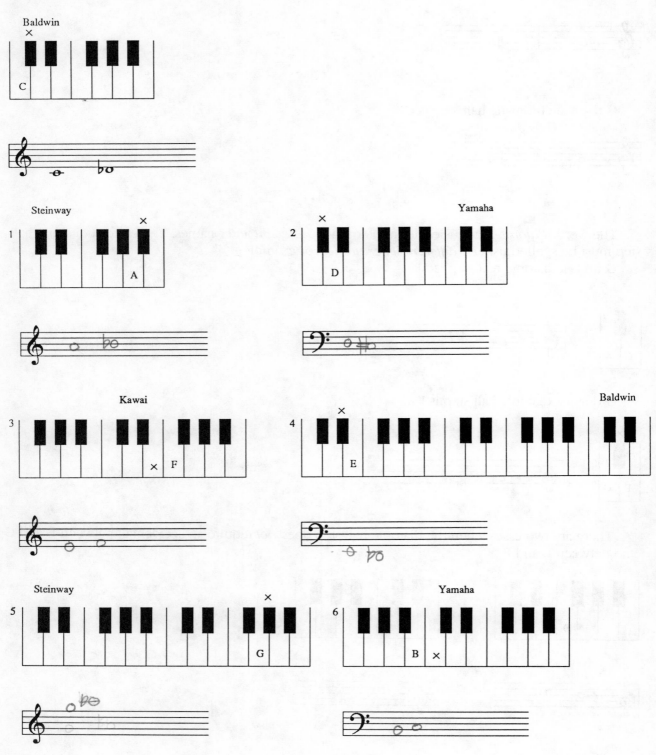

Diatonic Whole Steps

A diatonic whole step is simply two adjacent letter names that are two half-steps apart. For example:

 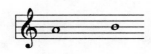

Diatonic whole steps occur naturally between every two adjacent letter names (A–B, C–D, D–E, F–G, and G–A) with two exceptions: B–C and E–F.

The distance between these pairs of notes (B–C and E–F) is a diatonic half-step. To make a diatonic whole step requires the use of an accidental. For example:

Creating a diatonic whole step between B and C:

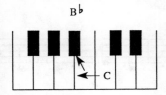 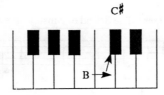

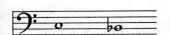 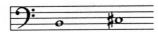

Creating a diatonic whole step between E and F:

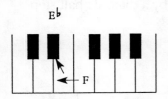 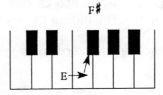

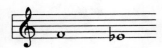 

Exercise 6

In the following songs a bracket is placed above certain adjacent letter names. Identify each as a diatonic half-step *(D ½)* or diatonic whole step *(D1)*. For example:

The Star Spangled Banner (traditional melody)

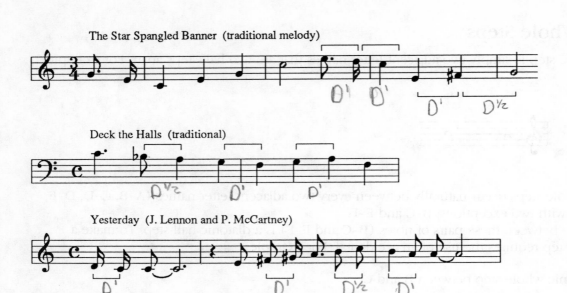

Deck the Halls (traditional)

Yesterday (J. Lennon and P. McCartney)

Climb Ev'ry Mountain (R. Rodgers: The Sound of Music)

Additional Exercises

Sight Singing Exercises

Exercise 1

Sing the following note groups consisting of a chromatic half step followed by a diatonic half step. Sing the letter names of the pitches (including the accidentals).

Instructor: Give the starting pitch of each three note group.

1

2

3

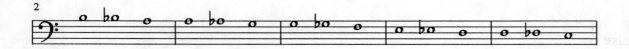

4

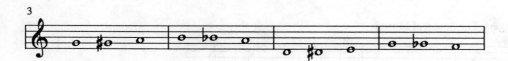

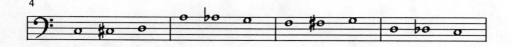

Keyboard Exercises

Exercise 1

Play each example three times to practice playing accidentals.

Other Exercises and Concepts

Writing Accidentals

The placement of symbols in our notaional system is extremely important. An incorrect placement may imply another meaning.

Accidentals are placed before a note *on the same line or space as the note head.*

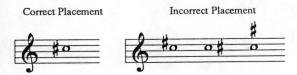

Exercise 1

Write the following notes (including accidentals) as indicated. Be conscious of the **placement** of the accidental. For example:

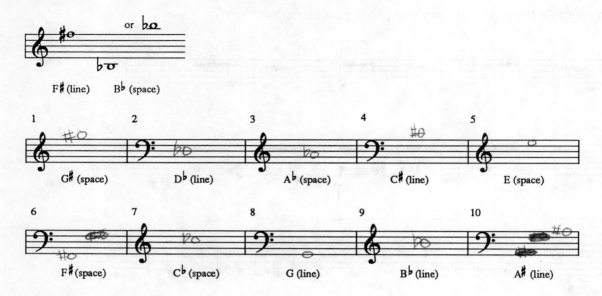

F♯ (line)   B♭ (space)

1   G♯ (space)   2   D♭ (line)   3   A♭ (space)   4   C♯ (line)   5   E (space)

6   F♯ (space)   7   C♭ (space)   8   G (line)   9   B♭ (line)   10   A♯ (line)

Exercise 2

Identify the following pitches. Place an X on the keyboard to show the **exact placement** of the note on the staff.

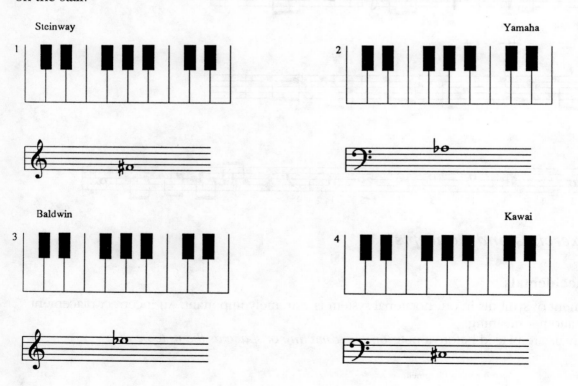

Steinway   Yamaha   Baldwin   Kawai

Steinway

5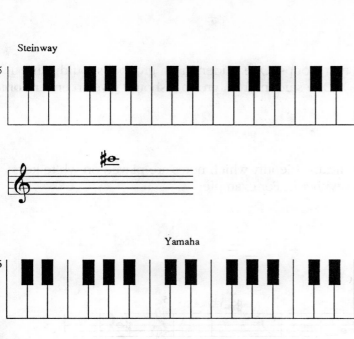

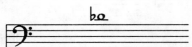

Yamaha

6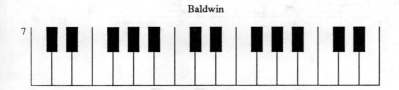

Baldwin

7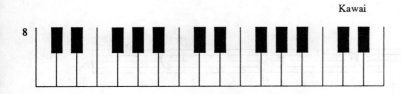

Kawai

8

Exercise 3

For class participation: Divide the class into two groups. One student from group 1 should name a pitch with a sharp or flat (for example F♯, A♭). One student from group 2 should give an enharmonic spelling of that pitch (F♯ = G♭, A♭ = G♯).

Exercise 4

Write each of the following pitches enharmonically. Identify which notes are played on white keys with a W and which are played on black keys with a B. For example:

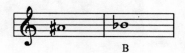

Exercise 5

Write the following diatonic half-steps up or down as indicated. For example:

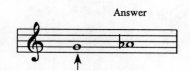

Double Sharps and Flats

Symbol	Name	Purpose
1. X	Double sharp	Raises a pitch one whole step (two ½ steps)

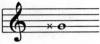

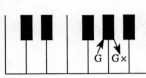

Symbol	Name	Purpose
2. ♭♭	Double flat	Lowers a pitch one whole step

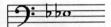

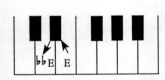

3. There is no double natural symbol. Only one natural is necessary to cancel a double sharp or double flat.

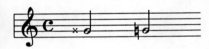

Exercise 6

Write the following pitches enharmonically. Identify which notes are played on white keys (W) and which are played on black keys (B) on the piano. For example:

Chapter 5 Major Scales

Let's now examine the last four measures of the song "Do Re Mi," concentrating only on the pitches.

Do re mi fa so la ti do

This is a series of diatonic pitches beginning and ending on the note C. This particular arrangement of tones is called a major scale.

Major Scales

The musical term *major* came into existence in the seventeenth century and is now used to distinguish scales, intervals (chapter 9), and chords (chapter 10). The major scale (Ionian mode) was actually one of eight medieval modes. Along with the Aeolian mode (chapter 7), it became one of the dominant scales by the eighteenth century.

A scale (from the Italian *scala,* meaning ladder) is tonal material arranged in an ascending or descending order. (There are many types of scales from various periods of music history as well as from different countries.)

If we analyze the distance between the successive pitches of the major scale, we will arrive at the following tonal relationship:

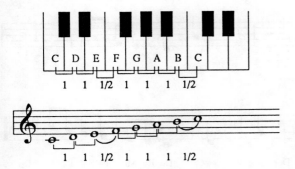

There are five diatonic whole steps (marked by 1s) and two diatonic half-steps (marked by ½s).

Properties of a Major Scale

1. A major scale is **diatonic.**
2. A major scale **begins** and **ends** on the same pitch.
3. A major scale has a tonal relationship of : 1 1 ½ 1 1 1 ½.

Scale steps are usually numbered 1–8; 8 is the starting pitch an octave higher.

1 2 3 4 5 6 7 8

Each tone of the scale has a name:

Tonic   Supertonic   Mediant   Subdominant   Dominant   Submediant   LeadingTone

Each tone of the scale also has a syllable attached to it:

Do Re Mi Fa So La Ti Do

This method of **solmization** (syllable singing) dates back to the eleventh century and was originated by Guido d'Arezzo. The syllables in the song "Do Re Mi" are a modern version of d'Arezzo's idea.

Doe   Ray   Me

Fa(r)   Sew   La

Tea   Doe   Do Re Mi Fa Sol La Ti Do

This major scale beginning on C contains only "natural" notes. It can be **transposed** (reproduced starting on a different pitch) without changing its **sound** by adhering to the properties of a major scale just listed.

Transposing the C major scale requires the use of accidentals. In each new version, the transposed scale will have the same sound since it maintains the same tonal relationship (1 1 ½ 1 1 1 ½).

Tetrachords

Before attempting to write a complete major scale beginning on pitches other than C, let's first learn to write a **tetrachord** (four diatonic pitches). A tetrachord can contain a variety of tonal relationships. We'll use the one characteristic of the major scale: 1 1 ½ (two diatonic whole steps followed by a diatonic half-step).
Example:

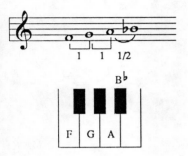

Exercise 1

In the following examples, add accidentals to make tetrachords with the tonal relationship 1 1 ½. Do not change the pitch of the first note. Use the keyboard to compute diatonic whole and half-steps.

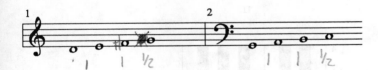

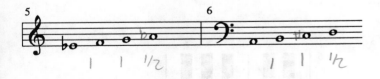

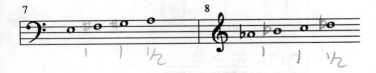

Exercise 2

Place **X**s on the keyboards in the following examples, showing the pitch of each note in the accompanying tetrachord.

Example:

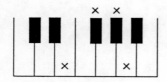

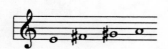

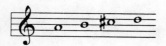

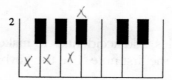

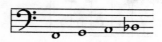

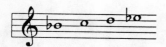

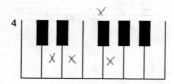

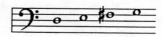

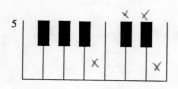

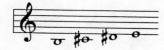

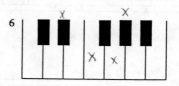

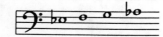

A major scale consists of *two tetrachords separated by a whole step.* Each tetrachord has the tonal relationship 1 1 ½.

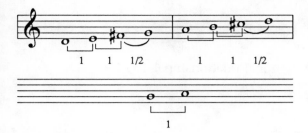

Two Methods for Writing a Major Scale

Instructors may choose one or use both methods.

Method 1 (Using the Tetrachord)

1. Write a tetrachord with the tonal relationship 1 1 ½. Since a tetrachord is diatonic, use four adjacent letter names.

2. From the last note of this tetrachord, write a diatonic whole step.

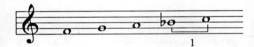

3. Beginning on this pitch, write another tetrachord with the tonal relationship 1 1 ½.

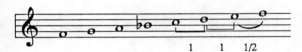

Method 2 (Using the Properties of a Major Scale)

1. Write a diatonic scale (seven adjacent letter names).

2. Add an eighth note the *same pitch* as the first (one octave higher).

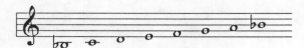

3. Adjust each pitch by the use of accidentals to make the tonal relationship 1 1 ½ 1 1 1 ½.

When you arrive at the final note of the scale, no additional adjustment will be necessary. (Step 2 has already made this note the correct pitch.) If a pitch adjustment *is* necessary you have made a mistake in the scale. Major scales *must* begin and end on the same pitch an octave apart.

Exercise 3

Write the following major scales using one of the methods just outlined. Use the keyboard to compute diatonic whole and half-steps.

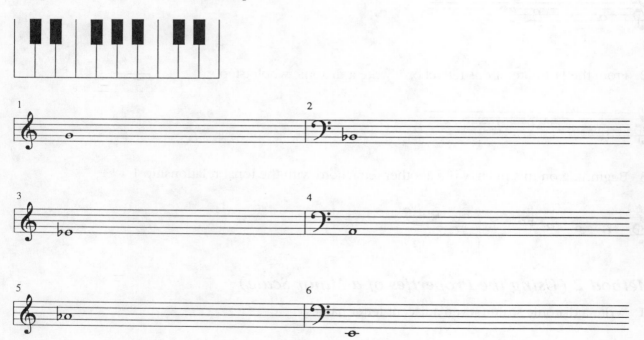

Exercise 4

Write the following major scales. Place **X**s on the keyboard to show the pitch of each note in the accompanying scale.

Example:

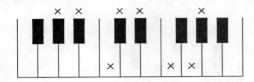

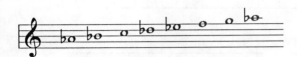

(Instructor: Play each scale in this exercise. Have students sing the scale in a comfortable range—an octave higher or lower. Use a neutral "ah" or the scale syllables previously mentioned.)

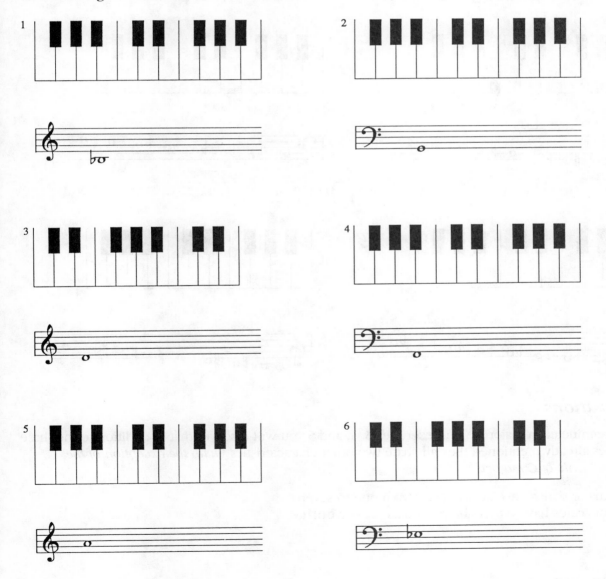

Exercise 5

Place an **X** on the given keyboard to show the pitch of each note in the following six scales. This exercise consists of three sets of **enharmonic** scales. Instructors should play the scales in pairs: 1 and 2; 3 and 4; and finally, 5 and 6. (The exercises in this text only require the knowledge of scales with up to four sharps or four flats. These scales are included to complete the series of the fifteen practical major scales.)

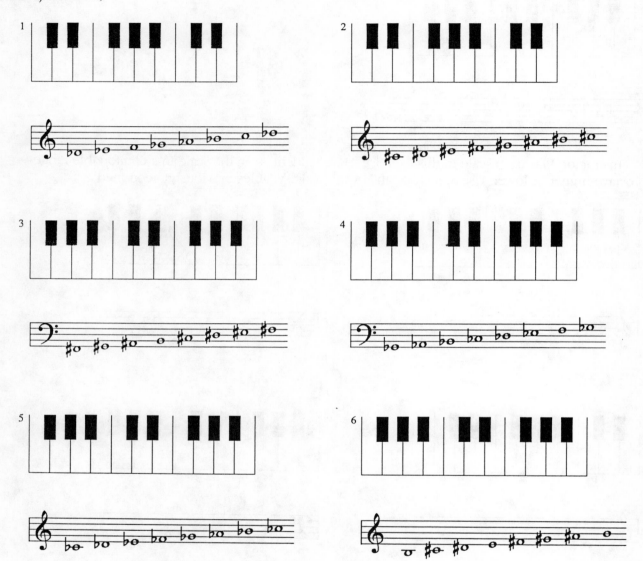

Observations

If you examine each major scale in exercises 3, 4, and 5 you will discover that in addition to the three properties already mentioned they all share two other characteristics (*with the exception of the "natural" scale of C major*):

1. All major scales have accidentals (from one to seven).
2. Major scales have either sharps *or* flats, **never both.**

Exercise 6

Each of the following scales are incorrect. Why?

Instructor: Play each of the scales and ask students which of them *sound* major.

Why do we use so many different major scales if they all have the same basic sound? Why not write every piece in the scale of C major with no accidentals? There are several possible reasons:

1. Probably the most obvious and valid reason is **range.** Try singing the following two versions of the "Star Spangled Banner":
   D Major Scale:

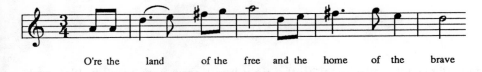

O're the   land   of the   free   and the   home   of the   brave

   This version is too high for most people to sing.
   A♭ Major Scale:

   This version is in a more comfortable range.

2. A more subtle reason is **tonal color.** This is more difficult to explain. Many composers develop feelings about certain scales. For example, D major is considered a "brighter" scale than A♭ major. (This concept can be traced back to the Greeks' doctrine of ethos.)

3. Finally, why *not* use the different scales? They are part of the musical language. Think of the English words that are synonymous with the word *beautiful:* lovely, pretty, gorgeous, attractive, and so on. We use these words because they add interest and variety to our language.

Additional Exercises

Sight Singing Exercises

Exercise 1

Sing the following major scales using the given syllables or an "ah" vowel. (Instructors should play each scale.) Which scale is the most comfortable for your voice?

Keyboard Exercises

Exercise 1

Play the following major scales. Play each scale first with the right hand, then with the left. Play each scale *slowly* using the correct fingerings.

C Major

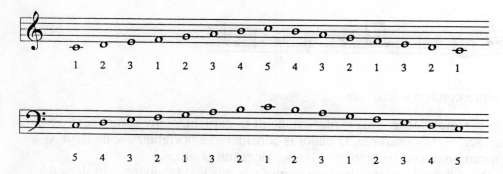

G Major

1 2 3 1 2 3 4 5 4 3 2 1 3 2 1

5 4 3 2 1 3 2 1 2 3 1 2 3 4 5

D Major

1 2 3 1 2 3 4 5 4 3 2 1 3 2 1

5 4 3 2 1 3 2 1 2 3 1 2 3 4 5

A Major

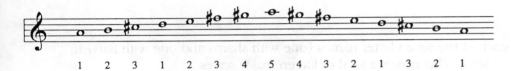

1 2 3 1 2 3 4 5 4 3 2 1 3 2 1

5 4 3 2 1 3 2 1 2 3 1 2 3 4 5

F Major

1 2 3 4 1 2 3 4 3 2 1 4 3 2 1

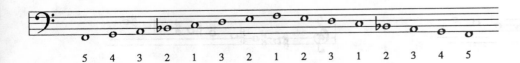

5 4 3 2 1 3 2 1 2 3 1 2 3 4 5

Bb Major

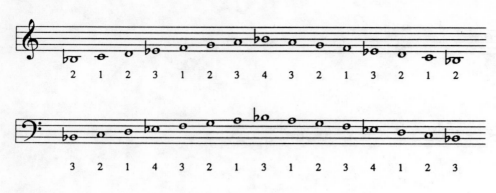

Eb Major

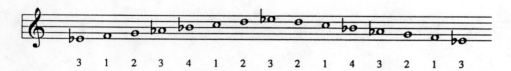

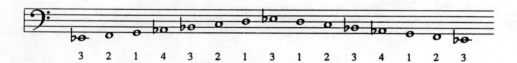

Additional Exercises and Concepts

Major Scales

There are two scales for each of the seven letter names (one with sharps and one with flats) in addition to the "natural" C scale. This makes a total of fifteen major scales.

Exercise 1

Below are the fifteen major scales arranged in pairs (there are three C scales). Write each set of scales, observing the relationship between each pair. Place an **X** on the keyboard to show the pitch of each note in the scale.
Example:

Scales on F

F Major

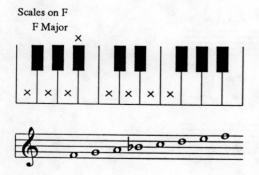

F# Major

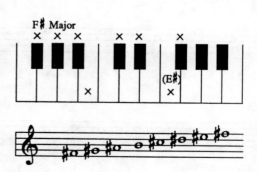

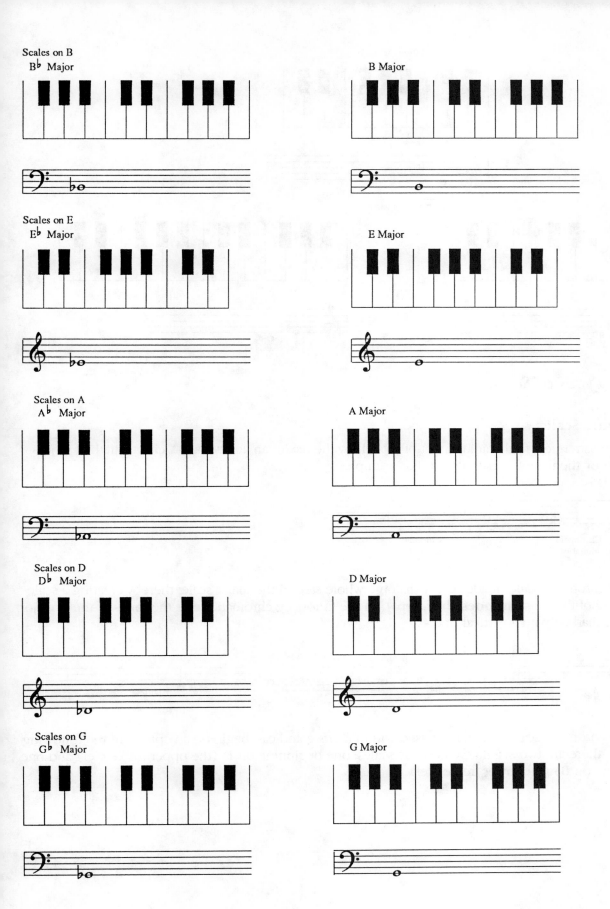

Scales on C (three scales)

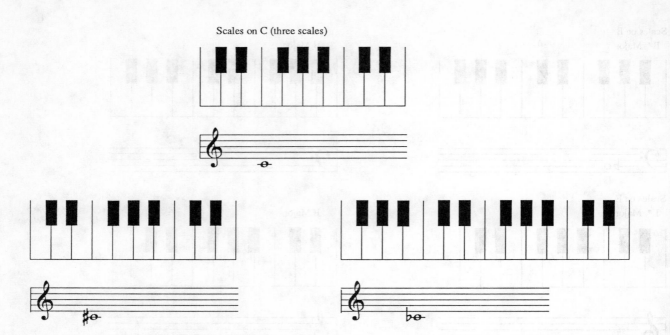

Other Types of Scales

Chromatic Scales

Chromaticism refers to the adjustment of a pitch by the use of an accidental. A chromatic half-step is achieved by the use of a sharp or flat. For example:

Chromatic   Chromatic
alteration   alteration

The chromatic scale divides every diatonic whole step in the major scale, thereby creating a scale consisting of twelve **semitones** (half-steps). In the following chromatic scale the tones of the C major scale are marked with a vertical line.

The chromatic scale is generally used within a piece and can begin on any pitch. In the following example there are two separate chromatic scales: one beginning on D (the upper treble clef) and one beginning on B♭ (the lower treble clef).

Hungarian Rhapsody No. 1 (F. Liszt)

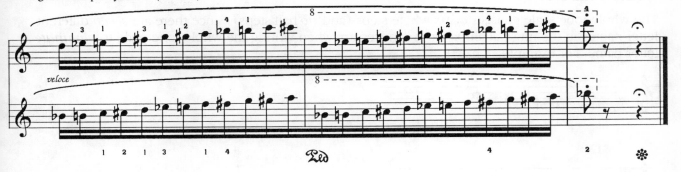

Exercise 2

In the preceding example, circle the notes of the D major scale in the upper clef and the notes of the
B♭ major scale in the lower clef.

Exercise 3

In each of the following examples, the notes of a major scale are placed in a square. Place an
accidental (♯, ♭, or ♮) in front of each of the remaining notes to make a chromatic scale. Use the
keyboard to compute chromatic half-steps.

Problem

Solution

Whole Tone Scales

The whole tone scale consists of *six* whole steps (and *no* half-steps). Since there are *seven* different letter names in the musical alphabet, it is necessary when writing the whole tone scale to *eliminate* a letter name. For example:

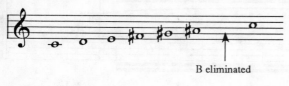

B eliminated

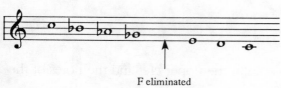

F eliminated

The whole tone scale may begin on any pitch. Example:

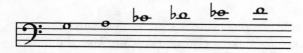

Claude Debussy used the whole tone scale in his piano piece "Reflects Dans L'eau" (Reflections in the Water).

Whole Tone Scale

Exercise 4

Place an accidental (♯ or ♭) in front of each of the following pitches (with the exception of the first pitch) to make whole tone scales.

1

2

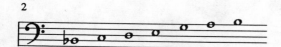

3

Pentatonic Scales

The pentatonic (five-tone) scale consists of five tones with the tonal relationship: 1   1 ½   1   1. It is sometimes thought of as the black key scale.

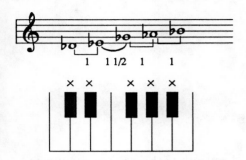

However, like other scales, the pentatonic scale can be transposed. For example:

This scale corresponds to the major scale with the elimination of scale steps three and seven.

Exercise 5

Place an accidental (♯ or ♭) in front of each of the following pitches to make a pentatonic scale with the tonal relationship 1   1 ½   1   1.

1

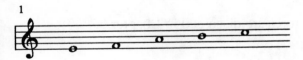

2

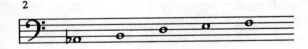

3

4

Although this is perhaps the most frequently used arrangement of tones for the pentatonic scale, other arrangements are possible by placing the one-and-a-half step interval in a different position.

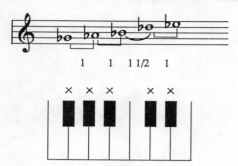

1   1   1 1/2   1

This version of the pentatonic scale (eliminating the fourth and seventh scale steps of the major scale) is used in many familiar melodies. Example:

Pentatonic Scale on F   F Major Scale

4   7   (1)

Auld Lang Syne (traditional melody)

This piece is written with a key signature. Key signatures are discussed in Chapter 6.

Church Modes

There are other scales (called **modes**) used in our notational system that originated in the medieval period of music history. Most of these ecclesiastical or church modes derive thier names from ancient Greece. (Even though the terminology has remained, church modes are not the same as the earlier Greek modes.) In the sixteenth century, the theorist Glareanus used the names **Ionian** and **Aeolian** to describe two church modes.

Each mode is shown here using only "natural" notes but, like other scales, every mode can be transposed. The transposition of any mode requires the use of accidentals.

The Ionian Mode
The Ionian mode consists of all of the white notes on the piano from C to C. (This scale corresponds to our present C major scale.)

1/2   1/2

The Dorian Mode

The Dorian mode consists of all of the white notes on the Piano from D to D.

The Phrygian Mode

The Phrygian mode consists of all of the white notes on the piano from E to E.

The Lydian Mode

The Lydian mode consists of all of the white notes on the piano from F to F.

The Mixolydian Mode

The Mixolydian mode consists of all of the white notes on the piano from G to G.

The Aeolian Mode

The Aeolian mode consists of all of the white notes on the piano from A to A. (This scale corresponds to our present A minor scale—see chapter 7.)

The Locrian Mode

The Locrian mode consists of all of the white notes on the piano from B to B.

Exercise 6

Write the following church modes beginning on the given pitch. Use the previous examples to find where the half-steps occur in each mode. (Like major scales, all of the church modes are **diatonic**.) Since the Ionian mode is the same as the major scale, it will not be used in this exercise. Example:

Chapter **6** *Key Signatures*

Let's now transpose the song "Do Re Mi" to the scale of A major.

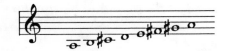

Since the tones F, C, and G are *always* sharp in the scale it's a waste of time to constantly write these accidentals. In order to simplify the notation, a **key signature** is used.

Key Signatures

A key signature is a symbol consisting of sharps *or* flats (never both) that tells which **tonality** (scale) a composer has chosen in which to write a muscial composition. The key signature is placed immediately *after* the clef sign and is repeated on every line of music. (The time signature is only written once.) For example:

Let's now write "Do Re Mi" using a key signature.

Doe, a deer a fe-male deer; Ray, a drop of gold-en sun;

Me, a name I call my-self; Fa(r). a long, long way to run;

Compare this version to the transposed version at the beginning of this chapter, which has no key signature. The key signature makes *writing* music easier, but it places a responsibility on the performer to *remember every accidental* in the key signature.

A key signature alters *every* pitch *named in the signature on any line or space* (including ledger lines) in the given clef. For example:

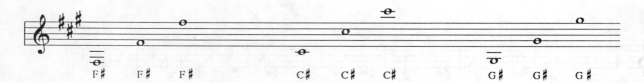

F♯ F♯ F♯   C♯ C♯ C♯   G♯ G♯ G♯

The Circle of Fifths

The circle of fifths, first described by J. D. Heinichen (c. 1728), shows the arrangement of the fifteen major scales in their order of increasing number of accidentals. The circle is to be read *clockwise* for the *sharp scales:*

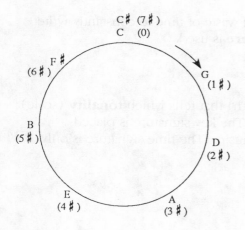

A linear representation may be easier to visualize:

Scale	C	G	D	A	E	B	F♯	C♯
Number of sharps	0	1	2	3	4	5	6	7

Observations

1. Letter names beginning at any given point on the circle are separated by a distance of five letters (hence the "circle of fifths").

   C   D   E   F   G   G   A   B   C   D   and so on
   1   2   3   4   5   1   2   3   4   5

2. The sharp scales all begin on *natural* letter names (G   D   A   E   B) with two exceptions (F♯ and C♯).

Exercise 1

Complete the circle of fifths for sharp scales.

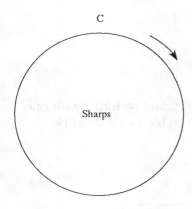

Complete this linear representation of the circle of fifths.
Sharps

C ——— C♯

0   1   2   3   4   5   6   7

Order of Accidentals in a Key Signature (Sharps)

The order of the accidentals in a *key signature* is *not* always the same as it is in the scale.

(The order is the same.)

(The order is different.)

The order of sharps in a key signature is *always:*

F♯, C♯, G♯, D♯, A♯, E♯, B♯

Accidentals in the key signature appear in the order in which they have been added with each successive scale.

Placement of Accidentals in a Key Signature (Sharps)

The placement of accidentals on the staff is very specific. Study the following example:

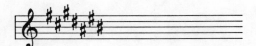

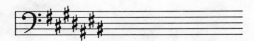

This is a repeating *down-up* pattern (that is, F♯ *down* to C♯, C♯ *up* to G♯, and so forth) with one exception (A♯). To avoid placing A♯ on a ledger line above the staff in the treble clef it must be placed on the second space.

Correct

Incorrect

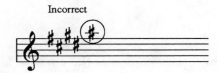

This placement is also used in the bass clef to keep the look of the key signature the same in both clefs.

Correct

Incorrect

Neither the *order* nor the *placement* of accidentals in a key signature can be altered.

Incorrect Order

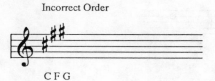

C F G

Incorrect Placement

F C G

These two examples do *not* show the key signature for A major even though they contain F, C, and G sharp. Key signatures must be "spelled" correctly (placed and ordered correctly).

Exercise 2

The following examples show the key signatures for the seven sharp keys. Copy the correct order and placement of sharps in the key signature.

1

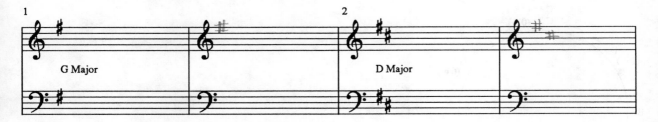

G Major

2

D Major

3

A Major

4

E Major

5

B Major

6

F# Major

7

C# Major

Flat Scales

The circle of fifths is read *counterclockwise* for *flat scales*:

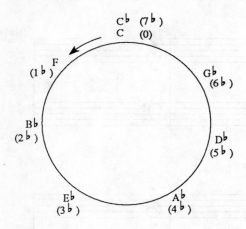

Again, a linear representation may be easier to visualize:

Scale	C	F	B♭	E♭	A♭	D♭	G♭	C♭
Number of flats	0	1	2	3	4	5	6	7
		B	E	A	D	G	C	F

Observations

1. The order of flats is *reversed* from that of sharps in the circle of fifths.
2. Letter names are separated by the distance of five letters when the musical alphabet is read *backwards*.

C	B	A	G	F		F	E	D	C	B
1	2	3	4	5		1	2	3	4	5

3. Flat scales all begin on flat notes (B♭, E♭, A♭, D♭, G♭, C♭) with one exception (F).

Exercise 3

Complete the circle of fifths for flat scales.

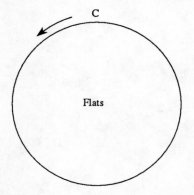

Complete this linear representation of the circle of fifths for flat scales.

Scale	C												Cb

Number of flats	0	1	2	3	4	5	6	7

Order of Accidentals in a Key Signature (Flats)

As in sharp key signatures, the order of the accidentals in a flat key signature is *not* always the same as it is in the scale.

(The order is the same.)

(The order is different.)

The order of flats in a key signature is:
Bb, Eb, Ab, Db, Gb, Cb, Fb
This is the *reverse* order of the sharps. The accidentals appear in the order in which they have been added with each successive scale.

Placement of Accidentals in a Key Signature (Flats)

Again, the placement of accidentals on the staff is very specific. Study the following example:

The pattern for flats is a repeating *up-down* pattern (that is, Bb *up* to Eb, Eb *down* to Ab). There is *no* alteration in the placement of flats. The pattern is the same for both the treble and bass clefs.

Neither the *order* nor the *placement* of accidentals in a key signature can be altered.

Incorrect Order   Incorrect Placement

E A B   B E A

These two examples do *not* show the key signature for E♭ major even though they contain B, E, and A flat.

Exercise 4

The following examples show the key signatures for the seven flat keys.
Copy the correct order and placement of flats in the key signature.

The key of C major has no accidentals and therefore no *apparent* key signature. For example:

Do Re Mi (R. Rodgers: The Sound of Music)

Exercise 5

Identify the following key signatures. (Refer to the circle of fifths.)

1. D Major
2.
3.
4. Ab Major
5.
6. Eb Major
7.
8. F Major

Exercise 6

Instructor: Divide the class into three groups. Name a key. Ask a student from Group 1 to identify the key as having sharps or flats; ask a student from Group 2 to give the number of accidentals; and ask a student from Group 3 to name the accidentals. (Student 3 should name the accidentals in the correct order in which they appear in the key signature.) Alternate groups.
Example:

Instructor	Student 1	Student 2	Student 3
D Major	Sharps	2	F and C

Exercise 7

Identify the major key signature for each of the following songs. Circle every note affected by the key signature. (A key signature alters every letter named in the signature on any line or space, including ledger lines.) Read the pitches in rhythm (excluding accidentals). Identify every rest and give its rhythmic (numerical) value. Which of these songs begins with an anacrusis? Sing each of the songs.

Home on the Range (D. Kelley and B. Higley)

F Major

Oh, give me a home where the buf-fa-lo roam where the deer and the an-te-lope play; where sel-dom is

heard a dis - cour - ag-ing word and the skies are not clou-dy all day.

Were You There? (spiritual)

Were you there when they cru-ci-fied my Lord? Were you there when they cru-ci-fied my Lord? Oh - - -

some-times it caus-es me to trem-ble trem-ble trem-ble. Were you there when they cru-ci-fied my Lord?

Shenandoah (traditional)

Oh, Shen-an-doah, I long to hear you. Way - hey, you roll-ing ri-ver. Oh, Shen-an-doah,

I long to hear you. Way, hey, we're bound a-way, 'cross the wide Mis - sou-ri.

Simple Gifts (Shaker song)

'Tis a gift to be sim-ple, 'tis a gift to be free, 'tis a gift to come down where you ought to be, and

when we find our-selves in a place just right, 'twill be in the val-ley of love and de-light.

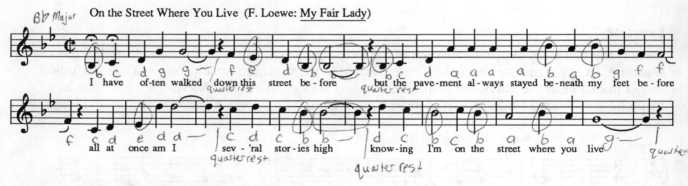

On the Street Where You Live (F. Loewe: <u>My Fair Lady</u>)

I have of-ten walked down this street be-fore but the pave-ment al-ways stayed be-neath my feet be-fore

all at once am I sev-'ral stor-ies high know-ing I'm on the street where you live

6. Good King Wenceslas (traditional)

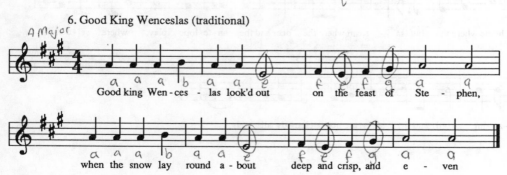

Good king Wen-ces - las look'd out on the feast of Ste - phen,

when the snow lay round a-bout deep and crisp, and e - ven

Exercise 8

Write the following major key signatures in *both clefs*.

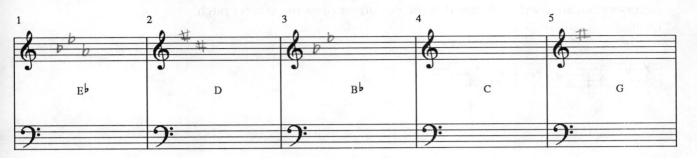

1. Eb
2. D
3. Bb
4. C
5. G

6. A
7. F
8. E
9. Ab

Added Accidentals

Earlier in this chapter we discovered that when accidentals are placed in a key signature they make every pitch with that letter name (in that clef) sharp or flat for the entire piece. This does *not* apply to accidentals added later in a piece.

An accidental placed before a note alters that pitch (on that line or space) for that entire measure. A bar line cancels any added accidental. For example:

When a note with an accidental is tied over a bar line, the accidental is also tied.

I Cain't Say No (R. Rodgers: Oklahoma!)

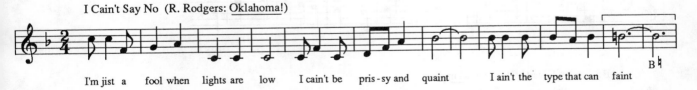

I'm jist a   fool when lights are   low   I cain't be pris-sy and quaint   I ain't the type that can   faint

"Safe" Accidentals

To avoid confusion many composers (and publishers) use "safe" accidentals. They are usually not necessary but are used to ensure that the performer plays the correct pitch.
Example:

"Safe" Accidental

In this example, the B in the second measure would be flat because the bar line cancels the natural sign.

Sometimes safe accidentals are added several measures later.
Example:

A Cock-Eyed Optimist (R. Rodgers: South Pacific)

Exercise 9

Discuss the safe accidentals in the following examples. Which accidentals **are** necessary?

I've Been Working on the Railroad (traditional)

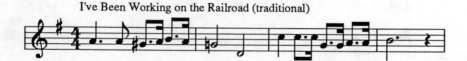

Break Forth, O Beauteous Heavenly Light (J. S. Bach)

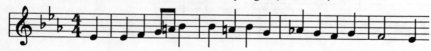

Verranno a Te (G. Donizetti: Lucia di Lammermoor)

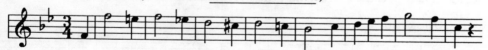

Bosom Buddies (J. Herman: Mame)

Additional Exercises

Sight Singing Exercises

Exercise 1

Identify the major key of each example. Then sing the melodies, using an "ah" vowel.

Keyboard Exercises

Exercise 1

Identify the major key signature of each of the following songs. Write the major scale, then pick out the melodies on the piano. Fill in the missing pitches *and* rhythms. (All pitches will belong to the major scale.) Circle all notes affected by the key signature.

Yankee Doodle (traditional)

Major Scale:

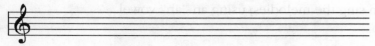

Exercise 2

Practice playing the major scales *slowly.* Each scales is written with a key signature. First play the right-hand part, then the left; then play both hands together. (The points at which you must change hand position are marked with a bracket.)

C Major

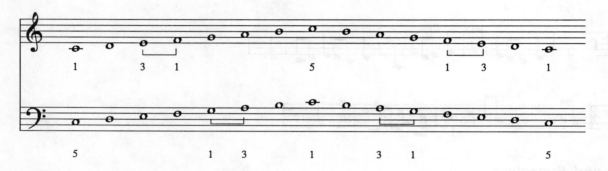

G Major

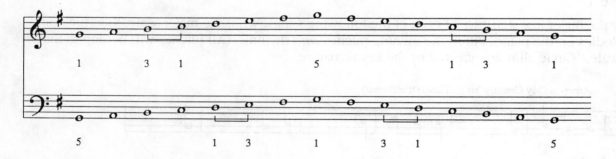

D Major

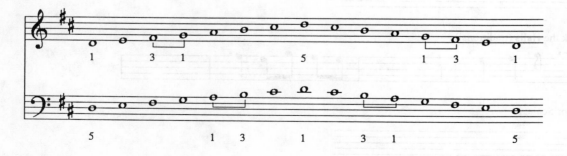

A Major

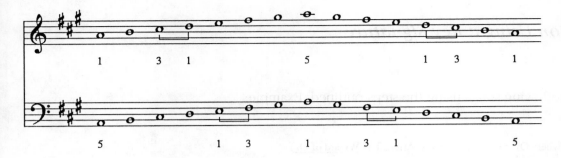

F Major

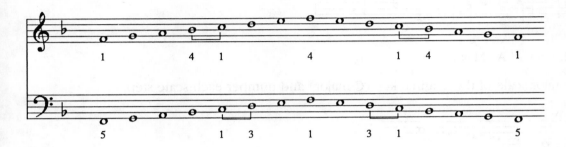

Bb Major

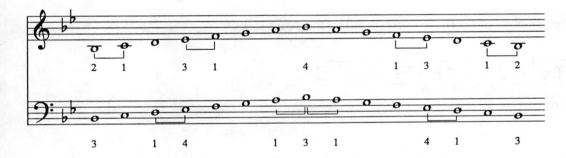

Eb Major

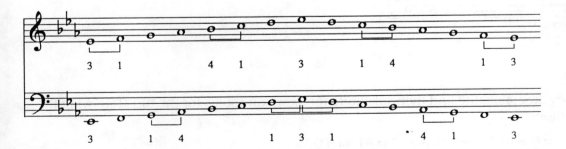

Other Exercises

Transposition Using a Key Signature

Exercise 1

Transpose the following songs using the steps outlined. Example:

Somewhere Over the Rainbow (H. Arlen: <u>The Wizard of Oz</u>)
Written in C Major

Transpose to the key of A♭ Major

1. Write the major scale of the original key (C major) and number each scale step.

2. Number the notes in the song to correspond to the scale steps.

3. Write the new key signature (A♭ major) and scale. Number the scale steps.

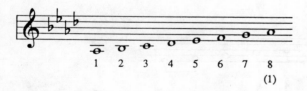

4. Write the new key signature and then substitute the new scale steps for the old (following the melodic contour).

Somewhere Over the Rainbow (H. Arlen: <u>The Wizard of Oz</u>)
Written in A♭ Major

Alouette (in G Major) (traditional)

Transpose to B♭ Major

G Major Scale   B♭ Major Scale

Alouette (in B♭ Major)

Around the World (in C Major) (V. Young)

Transpose to E♭ Major

C Major Scale   E♭ Major Scale

Around the World (in E♭ Major)

Jingle Bells (in D Major) (J. Pierpont)

Transpose to G Major

D Major Scale   G Major Scale

Jingle Bells (in G Major)

Chapter 7 *Minor Keys*

Let's examine the love theme from the movie *Romeo and Juliet.* A Time for Us (N. Rota)

At first glance, this song may look like any other piece we have studied. It is written in the treble clef, has a time signature of **3/4** , begins with an anacrusis, and has a key signature with no accidentals.

Since this piece has a key signature with no accidentals, we would expect it to be written in the key of C major. However, the piece begins and ends on the note A. This piece is written in the key of **A minor** (the Aeolian mode—see chapter 5, Additional Exercises).

Minor Keys

Minor keys share key signatures with major keys because in their *pure* forms they contain the same pitches. (The "forms" of the minor keys will be discussed later in this chapter.) A different **arrangement** of pitches creates a different **sound** (because of the new placement of the half-steps). [Instructor's should play the C Major and A Minor (pure form) scales].

Perhaps a simple analogy will help explain the distinction between major and minor keys: The words *step* and *pest* both contain the same letters, but arranging those letters differently creates a different **sound** and, consequently, a different **meaning.**

Relative Major and Minor Keys

Major and minor keys that share the same key signature are called **relative** keys. Every major key has a relative minor key. The *order* and *placement* of the accidentals in the key signature is exactly the same in a minor key as it is in the relative major key.

Identifying Minor Key Signatures

To identify the minor key that shares the major key signature use the following steps.
Problem: Identify the following minor key signature.

Solution:
1. Identify the major key signature (four sharps is the key of E major).
2. From the starting pitch of the *major* key (in this case, E) go *down three* letter names (or *up six* letter names).

3. Check the key signature to see if this note has been altered. This pitch, altered or unaltered, signifies the relative minor key.

   C is sharp in the key signature. Therefore, the relative minor key of E major is C♯ minor.

Exercise 1

Identify the following minor key signatures using the three steps just outlined.

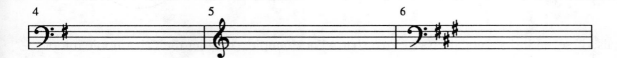

Three Forms of the Minor

Minor keys have three forms:

1. Pure (natural)
2. Harmonic
3. Melodic

Major scales have no such distinction.

The key signature for all three of these forms is *exactly the same*. Any pitch alterations are made within the scale (or piece).

Pure (Natural) Minor

The pure (natural) minor has *no* alterations from the key signature. For example:
Scale: A Minor (pure or natural)

Musical Example:

A Time for Us (N. Rota)

Harmonic Minor

In the natural minor, the seventh scale step is a diatonic whole step below the tonic (the starting pitch of the scale). The harmonic minor changes this distance to a diatonic half-step to create a "pull" toward the tonic. The harmonic minor therefore has a **raised seventh scale step.** For example:
Scale: G Minor (Harmonic)

Raised Seventh

Musical Example:

Coventry Carol (traditional)

A "raised" seventh does not always mean a sharp. For example, consider the C harmonic minor scale:

Scale: C Minor (Harmonic)

Raised Seventh

Musical Example:

Piano Sonata Op. 10 No. 1 (L. van Beethoven)

Melodic Minor

By raising the seventh scale step in the harmonic minor, we have created a distance of one and one-half steps between the sixth and seventh scale steps. For example:

Scale: D Minor (Harmonic)

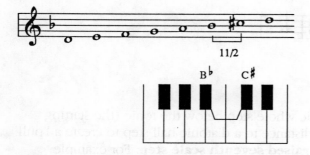

11/2

B♭ C♯

To create a smoother progression of tones, the melodic minor also raises the **sixth** scale step when ascending:

On the other hand, both the sixth and seventh scale steps are **lowered** when descending:

The descending melodic minor scale is identical to the natural minor scale.
Musical Example:

Don Giovanni (Overture) (W.A. Mozart)

Some pieces fluctuate between these three forms of the minor. Many pieces even alternate between major and minor keys.

(In all of the exercises in this book, examples will be either in a major key or a minor key. Any example in a minor key will be in only one form of the minor.)

Comparing Major and Minor Scales

Major and natural minor scales contain sharps *or* flats, *never both.*
Example:

Harmonic and melodic minor scales may contain *both* sharps and flats. Alterations are made in the scale or piece, but *not in the key signature*.

G Harmonic Minor

D Melodic Minor

Exercise 2

Instructor: Play major and natural minor scales and ask the students to identify them by sound.

Exercise 3

Instructor: Play only minor scales and ask the students to identify the form of the minor scale: natural, harmonic, or melodic.
Students: The harmonic minor scale has a unique sound: the distance of the one and one-half steps between scale steps 6 and 7. The melodic minor sounds different descending and ascending.

Distinguishing between Major and Minor Scales (Key Signatures)

You may be wondering: If every major key has a relative minor key with the same key signature, how do you know *which* key a piece is written in? For example:

This is the key signature for both G major *and* E minor (natural, harmonic, and melodic). To find which of these four scales is being used, you must look at the arrangement of pitches in the piece.

In any scale (major or minor), the two most important tones are the tonic (starting pitch) and the dominant (fifth scale step).

G Major   E Minor

The tonic and dominant tones for *all three forms* of the minor are exactly the same.

Musical Analysis

In analyzing a piece, you will find that *generally* the melody will gravitate around the tonic and dominant tones. (Although melodic contour is not always an indication of tonality, in this text all examples will follow this general rule.)

My Favorite Things (R. Rodgers: <u>The Sound of Music</u>)

This example gravitates around the tones E and B (the tonic and dominant of the key of E minor).

Alouette (traditional)

This example gravitates around the tones G and D (the tonic and dominant of the key of G major).

Simple melodies usually begin and end on the tonic. However, many songs begin on the third or fifth of the scale.

Jingle Bells (J. Pierpont)

This example begins on the third of the A♭ major scale.

Carol of the Birds (Spanish carol)

This example begins on the fifth of the F minor scale.

Major or Minor?

To discover whether a piece is written in the major or relative minor, use the following steps.
Problem: Decide the key of the following musical example.

Symphony No. 5 (Third Movement) (F. Schubert)

Solution:

1. Decide the possibilities. Two flats is the key signature for B♭ major and G minor.

2. Write the tonic tone of the major key, then count up five letter names to the dominant. Do the same for the minor.

B♭ Major   G Minor

1   5   1   5

3. Examine the pitches in the melody and decide which set of tonic-dominant tones is the most important.

G Minor   5   1   5   1   5   5   5   5

B♭ Major   1   1

This piece is written in G minor because it gravitates around G and D. We can tell it is not in B♭ major because of the absence of the dominant tone in that key. *It is important to hear the dominant going to the tonic at some point in the melody.*

Distinguishing the Three Forms of the Minor

Once you have decided that a piece is in a minor key you must decide which **form** of the minor (natural, harmonic, or melodic) it takes.

1. If there are no alterations, the form is **natural.**
2. If only the seventh scale step is raised, the form is **harmonic.**
3. If the sixth and seventh scale steps are raised when ascending and lowered when descending, the form is **melodic.**

Exercise 4

Identify the key of each of the following melodies (major, natural minor, harmonic minor, or melodic minor). All the examples are in only one key, and the minor keys are in only one form.

    Below each example write both the major and the relative minor scales and identify the tonic and dominant of each.

Instructor: Play each example.

Overture (R. Wagner: <u>Die Meistersinger</u>)

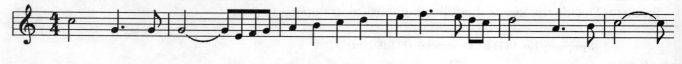

Finch' han dal vino (W. A. Mozart: Don Giovanni)

You Are the Sunshine of My Life (S. Wonder)

O Come, O Come Emmanuel (plainsong melody)

Ode to Joy (L. van Beethoven: Symphony No. 9)

Nina (L. V. Ciampi; attributed to G. B. Pergolesi)

Bridge Over Troubled Water (P. Simon)

Piano Sonata Op. 13 (Third Movement) (L. van Beethoven)

Additional Exercises

Sight Singing Exercises

Exercise 1

Decide in which form of the minor each example is written. Then sing the melodies using an "ah" vowel.

Keyboard Exercises

Exercise 1

Play the following harmonic minor scales. Play each scale *slowly,* and play the hands *separately.*

A Minor

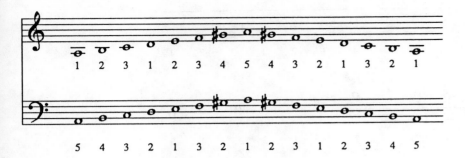

1 2 3 1 2 3 4 5 4 3 2 1 3 2 1

5 4 3 2 1 3 2 1 2 3 1 2 3 4 5

E Minor

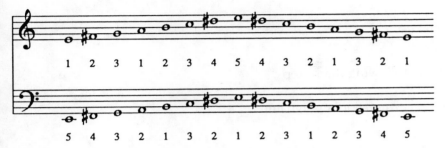

1 2 3 1 2 3 4 5 4 3 2 1 3 2 1

5 4 3 2 1 3 2 1 2 3 1 2 3 4 5

B Minor

1 2 3 1 2 3 4 5 4 3 2 1 3 2 1

4 3 2 1 4 3 2 1 2 3 4 1 2 3 4

D Minor

1 2 3 1 2 3 4 5 4 3 2 1 3 2 1

5 4 3 2 1 3 2 1 2 3 1 2 3 4 5

G Minor

1 2 3 1 2 3 4 5 4 3 2 1 3 2 1

5 4 3 2 1 3 2 1 2 3 1 2 3 4 5

C Minor

Other Exercises

Writing Minor Key Signatures

Problem:

To write a minor key signature use the following three steps.

Write the key signature for G minor.

Remember: Every minor scale has a relative major key signature.

Solution:

1. Write the tonic of the minor scale (the *name* of the minor key: in this case G).

2. Go *up* three half-steps.

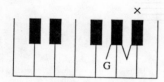

This pitch is A♯ or B♭. Since the correct *spelling* of this pitch must be three *letter names* from the starting pitch, the correct spelling is B♭.

3. This tone is the starting pitch of the relative major.
   G minor, therefore, has the same key signature as B♭ major.

Exercise 1

Write the following minor key signatures using the three steps just outlined.

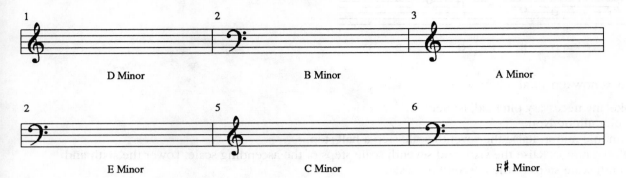

1	2	3
D Minor	B Minor	A Minor

2	5	6
E Minor	C Minor	F♯ Minor

It is very easy to get confused about the direction used to identify or write minor key signatures. When do I go up? When down?

Memorize *one* example of relative keys to help you remember:

C Major
A Minor

What is the key signature for D minor?

? Major
D Minor (Go *up* from the minor)

B♭ major has the same key signature as what minor key?

B♭ Major
? Minor (Go *down* from the major)

Writing Minor Scales

To write a minor scale, use the following steps:
Problem: Write a C harmonic minor scale.
Solution:

1. Write the key signature of the relative major key.

? Major
C Minor (Go *up*)

C minor has the same key signature as E♭ major: three flats (B♭, E♭, and A♭).

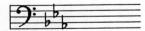

2. Write a diatonic scale beginning on the letter name of the minor scale (in this case C).

        C   D   E   F   G   A   B   C

This is now a natural minor scale.

3. Make any necessary pitch adjustment.
Natural minor: None
Harmonic minor: Raise the seventh scale step a half-step.
Melodic minor: Raise the sixth and seventh scale steps of the ascending scale. Lower the sixth and seventh scale steps of the descending scale.

Since we want a harmonic minor scale, we must raise the seventh scale step a half-step.

Exercise 2

Write the following minor scales.

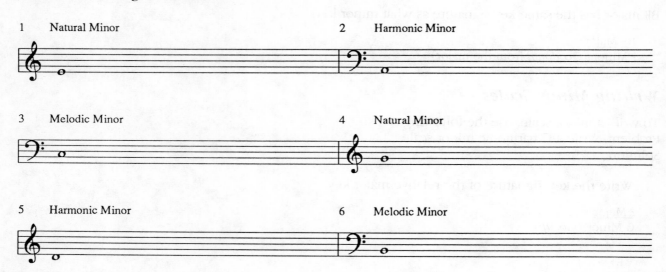

1   Natural Minor   2   Harmonic Minor

3   Melodic Minor   4   Natural Minor

5   Harmonic Minor   6   Melodic Minor

Chapter 8 Compound Meters

In chapter 7 we mentioned that it is possible for a composition to fluctuate between the three forms of the minor as well as between major and minor keys. In the song "Greensleeves" ("What Child is This?") the sixth scale step is raised every time it is used (indicating the melodic minor). However, the seventh scale step is not raised until measure 7. In measures 9–14 there is a brief departure to the relative major (G major). In the final two measures (15 and 16), the melody returns to the tonal center of E minor.

Greensleeves (traditional)

This piece is interesting not only for its changing tonal center but also for its meter. If we look closely at the time signature (6/8) and the way the notes are beamed ( ), we will see that this piece is different from any other we have studied.

At first glance, it would seem that the meaning of the 6/8 meter is that there are six beats in a measure and that the eighth note ( ) is the pulse note. However, in the first measure we see that three notes are beamed together to form the pulse note. This is an example of **compound meter.**

Compound Meters

Compound meters are meters that have *dotted notes as pulse notes.* Dotted notes can be divided evenly into three notes:

The *bottom number* in a compound meter represents the *division* of the pulse note (not the pulse note). (The reason for this is that dotted notes cannot be expressed with a number. The symbol

is a dotted quarter note, not a "3" or "third" note.) The beat is still grouped in duple, triple, or quadruple time.

Since the bottom number represents the division of the pulse, the *top number* in a compound meter is three times larger than the normal grouping. For example, in duple meter the top number is 6 (not 2); in triple meter the top number is 9 (not 3); and in quadruple meter the top number is 12 (not 4).

In compound meters, *any* dotted note may be used as the pulse note; however, the dotted quarter is the most frequently used. We will limit our musical examples in this section to the following time signatures:

$\frac{6}{8}$ $\frac{9}{8}$ $\frac{12}{8}$

Rests

Rests may be dotted in either simple or compound meters. Some composers choose to write two separate rests instead of a dotted rest, especially with the whole and half rests. Either method is acceptable.

Beaming

Notes are beamed together in compound meters for the same reasons they are beamed in simple meters.

1. To make the pulse note

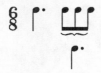

Notes of different values may be beamed together to form the pulse note. For example:

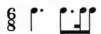

2. To make a division of the pulse note

Rhythmic Patterns

The following are a few of the most frequently used rhythmic patterns in compound meter.

Dotted Quarter Note as the Pulse Note

When the dotted quarter note is the pulse note, the time signatures may be any of the following:

$$\frac{6}{8} \qquad \frac{9}{8} \qquad \frac{12}{8}$$

Patterns

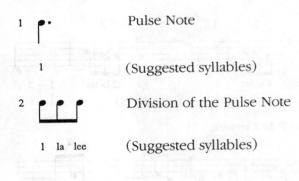

Exercise 1

Tap or clap a beat. Sing one measure in a $\frac{12}{8}$ meter (four beats per measure) using Pattern 1 (the dotted quarter note as the pulse note).

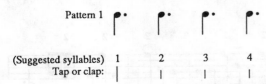

Tap or clap a beat. Sing one measure in a **12/8** meter using Pattern 2 (the division of the pulse note).

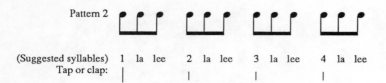

| (Suggested syllables) | 1 | la | lee | 2 | la | lee | 3 | la | lee | 4 | la | lee |
| Tap or clap: | | | | | | | | | | | | | | | | |

Tap or clap a beat. Sing one measure in a **12/8** meter using Pattern 3 (the subdivision of the pulse note).

| (Suggested syllables) | 1 ta la ta lee ta | 2 ta la ta lee ta | 3 ta la ta lee ta | 4 ta la ta lee ta |
| Tap or clap: | | | | | | | | |

Exercise 2

The following pieces contain these three patterns in addition to notes that are longer than the pulse note. Sing the rhythm (using the suggested syllables), visualizing the patterns. Tap or clap a beat. (If a piece contains ties and/or rests, sing the pattern first without the tie or rest, then again observing the tie or rest.)

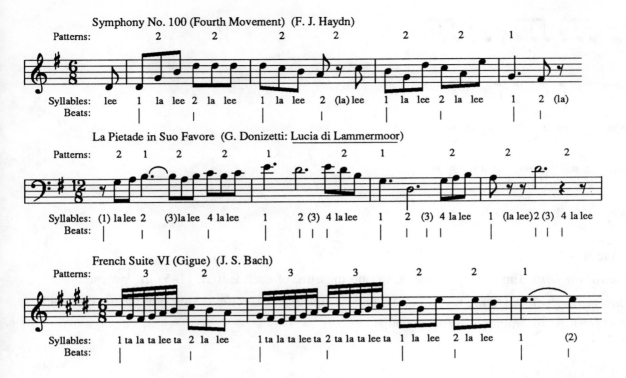

If you study a few basic patterns, you will soon be able to see variations of those patterns and identify them quickly.

In the English language, we can usually see the basic word from which other words have been derived: *musical* and *musician* both come from *music*.

In music,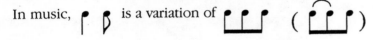

Variations of Pattern 2

2
1   la   lee

4
1   lee

5
1   la

Exercise 3

Individual students: Tap or clap a beat. Sing one measure in $\frac{12}{8}$ meter using Pattern 4. (Repeat, using Pattern 5.)

For class participation: Divide the class into two groups. Group 1: Tap or clap a beat. Group 2: Tap or clap the division of the beat (Pattern 2). *Everyone:* Sing one measure in a $\frac{12}{8}$ meter, using Pattern 4. Repeat, using Pattern 5. Alternate groups.

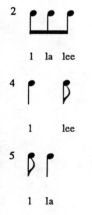

Group 1
Tap or clap:

Compound Meters

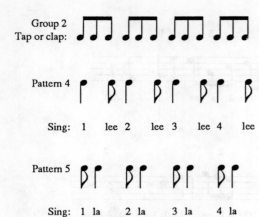

Group 2
Tap or clap:

Pattern 4

Sing: 1   lee   2   lee   3   lee   4   lee

Pattern 5

Sing: 1   la   2   la   3   la   4   la

Exercise 4

Individual students: Tap or clap a beat. Sing one measure of each Pattern (1–5) in $\frac{12}{8}$ meter.

For class participation: Divide the class into two groups as in exercise 3. Sing one measure of each pattern (1–5) in $\frac{12}{8}$ meter. Alternate groups.

Group 1
Tap or clap:

Group 2
Tap or clap:

Pattern 1

Sing: 1   2   3   4

Pattern 2

Sing: 1   la   lee   2   la   lee   3   la   lee   4   la   lee

Pattern 3

Sing: 1 ta la ta lee ta   2 ta la ta lee ta   3 ta la ta lee ta   4 ta la ta lee ta

Pattern 4

Sing: 1   lee   2   lee   3   lee   4   lee

Pattern 5

Sing: 1   la   2   la   3   la   4   la

Exercise 5

The following pieces contain Patterns 1, 2, 4, and 5 in addition to notes that are longer than the pulse note. Tap a beat. Sing the rhythm (using the suggested syllables), visualizing the patterns. (Pattern numbers are written above each example. Discover which patterns are the most difficult for you and review them in the previous exercises.)

Dotted Patterns

Although there are many possibilities using dotted patterns, we will limit our discussion to only one.

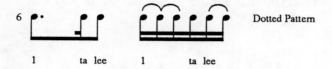

Exercise 6

Individual students: Tap or clap a beat. Sing one measure in $\frac{12}{8}$ meter using Pattern 6.

For class participation: Divide the class into three groups. Group 1: Tap or clap a beat. Group 2: Tap or clap the division of the beat (Pattern 2).

Group 3: Tap or clap the subdivision of the beat (Pattern 3). Everyone: Sing one measure in $\frac{12}{8}$ meter using Pattern 6. Alternate groups.

Exercise 7

The following pieces contain pattern 6 (in addition to the patterns previously studied). Tap a beat. Sing the rhythm (using the suggested syllables), visualizing the patterns. (Pattern numbers are written above each example.)

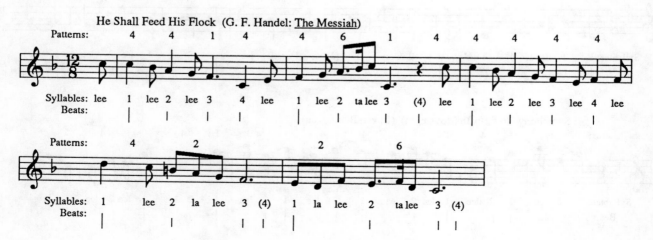

Triplets

We are now acquainted with the two types of meters used in our system: simple and compound. In simple meters, the pulse note can be divided evenly into two notes (♩ = ♫). In compound meters the pulse note can be divided equally into three notes (♩. = ♪♪♪).

It is possible to "borrow" a division of the pulse note from a simple meter and use it in a compound meter. When this borrowing takes place, we refer to the division as a triplet. *A triplet divides a note that is normally divided into two even notes into three even notes.*

Example:

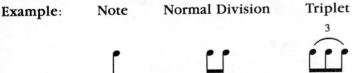

Note	Normal Division	Triplet

The three notes marked as a triplet equal two of the same type of note. Some musicians incorrectly refer to the normal division of the pulse in compound meter as a triplet. However, in compound meter the normal division of the pulse *is* three. A triplet is not just a division by three but a division by three that is normally a division by two.

Exercise 8

In the following examples substitute a triplet for each normal division of the pulse note.
Example:

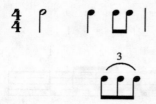

Exercise 9

Each of the following examples contains a triplet. Sing the rhythm of each song, using the suggested syllables. (If necessary, write the syllables under each note).

Feelings (M. Albert)

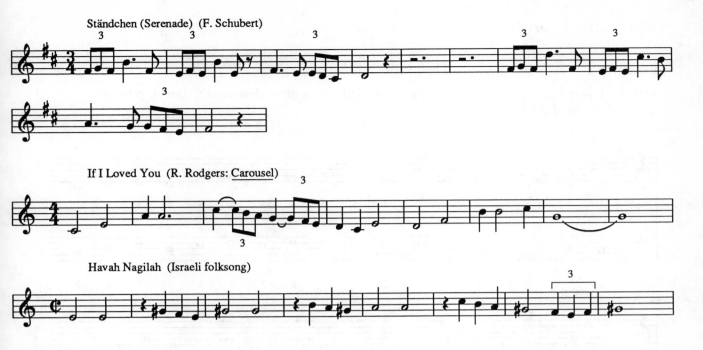

Additional Exercises

Sight Singing Exercises

Exercise 1

Sing the rhythm of the following pieces. Then sing only the pitches (using an "ah" vowel or the suggested syllables). Finally, sing the example with both pitch and rhythm.

Keyboard Exercises

Exercise 1

Play the following exercises using both hands. This exercise is designed to develop finger independence and hand coordination.

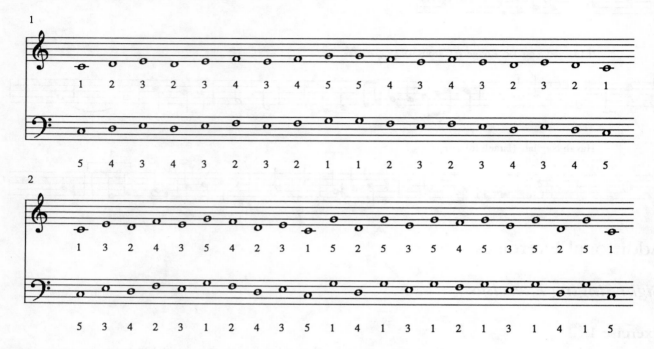

Exercise 2

Play the following exercises in compound meters. Practice each hand separately, then play with both hands. Sing the rhythm (using syllables) as you play.

Chapter 8

Other Exercises

Exercise 1

The following songs are in compound meters. Rewrite each song. Add beams where possible and bar lines where necessary. (When a song begins with an anacrusis the first bar line is given.) Sing each song, first looking at the original version, then at the new "beamed" version. (In each of the examples the pulse note is the dotted quarter.)

Exercise 2

Instructor: Ask one member of the class to tap or clap a beat and sing four patterns. The rest of the class must decide which patterns were sung. (Patterns may be repeated.)
Example:

(The singer **must** strive to perform the rhythmic patterns *accurately* in four steady beats.)

Students can decide on their own four patterns or choose from one of the following:

Duplets

It is also possible to "borrow" a division of the pulse note from a compound meter and use it in a simple meter. When this takes place, we refer to the division as a **duplet**. *A duplet divides a note that is normally divided into three even notes into two even notes.*

Example:

Note   **Normal Division**   **Duplet**

The two notes marked as a duplet equal three of the same type of note.

Andrew Lloyd Webber used duplets in the song "Memory" from the hit musical *Cats*.

Memory (A. L. Webber: <u>Cats</u>)

<h1 style="text-align: center;">Chapter 9 Intervals</h1>

In chapter 4 (exercise 6), we measured the distance between adjacent tones (diatonic half-step and diatonic whole step).

For example:

Do Re Mi (R. Rodgers: <u>The Sound of Music</u>)

Now let's consider measuring the distance between any two pitches.

Intervals

The distance between two pitches is called an **interval.** These pitches may be successive (melodic interval):

or simultaneous (harmonic interval).

When notes are placed above one another on the staff they sound simultaneously.
The process for measuring melodic and harmonic intervals is the same.

The Purpose of Intervals

Musicians use intervals for three main purposes:

1. To identify (name) distances.
2. To show the relationship between two pitches.
3. As a method of ear training. Musicians memorize the sound of every interval in order to sing that interval or recognize it when it is played.

Interval Identification

Because intervals are distances that involve measurement, their identification is mathematical. Intervals are identified by their *quantity* (number) and *quality* (distance or size).

Let's think for a moment in mathematical terms. Each of the following lines is identified in relation to a measurement of two inches, but they are all different sizes:

_____ 2 inches

_____ 2¼ inches

_____ 2½ inches

In music we use a similar system of identification in measuring the distance between pitches:

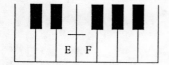 E-F (1/2 step)

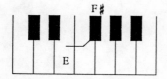 E-F♯ (1 step)

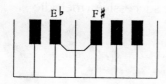 E♭-F♯ (1 1/2 step)

Each of these three examples involves two adjacent letter names. However, because of the accidentals, the actual *distance* between each pair of pitches is different. With this concept in mind let's discuss a method for identifying intervals.

Identifying Interval Quantity

The quantity of an interval is determined by the number of consecutive *letter names* involved between the two pitches. The *first* and *last* letter names are always included in the counting. Example:

```
C to F is a fourth.          G to D is a fifth.
C D E F                           G A B C D
1 2 3 4                           1 2 3 4 5
```

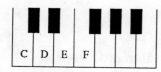

Identifying Interval Quality

The quality of an interval is the actual number of half-steps between two pitches. In the song "Do Re Mi" the distance between C and E, and the distance between D and F, is a third.

However, the sizes of these thirds differ because of the number of half-steps between each of the pitches:

Four half-steps

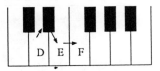

Three half-steps

In measuring small distances it is easy to count scale steps; however, as intervals become larger, counting half-steps becomes more time consuming. This method of computing intervals requires the memorization of various combinations of numbers.

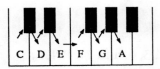

Six Letter Names (Nine half-steps)

Seven Letter Names (Eleven half-steps)

Let's use a *key signature approach* that will prove less mathematical and at the same time allow us to make practical use of the knowledge we acquired in chapter 6 ("Major Key Signatures").

Identifying Intervals: Key Signature Approach

Premise

In any major scale the distance from the starting pitch to scale steps 2, 3, 6, and 7 is called *major*. (See chapter 5.)
C Major Scale (M = Major)

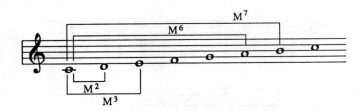

Major Intervals:

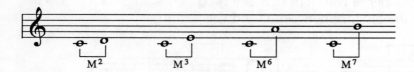

(A major second is a diatonic whole step.)

D Major Scale

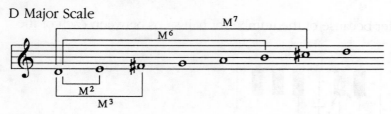

Major Intervals:

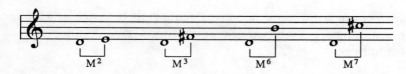

Exercise 1

Write the following major scales; then write and identify all major intervals (2, 3, 6, and 7). Refer to the examples just studied.

"Quality Adjustment" of Major Intervals

Minor Intervals

Any major distance made smaller by a half-step is called *minor*. (The number of half-steps in each interval is given below each example.)

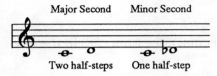

A minor second is a diatonic half step.

Method of Interval Identification

Two aspects of an interval must be identified: the "quantity" of the interval and the "quality" of the interval.

Problem: Identify the following interval.

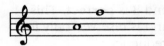

Solution:

1. To find the quantity: Count the letter names (including the starting and ending pitches. In this example, the distance from A to F is a sixth.

   A B C D E F

   1 2 3 4 5 6

2. To find the quality: Apply the key signature of the bottom note. (Instead of writing a complete major scale, apply the key signature of the bottom note to see if the upper note fits in the scale.)

F C G

In our example of the interval from A to F, the upper note F (natural) does *not* "fit" in the key signature of A major.

3. Compare: If the upper note fits in the key signature (scale), then the interval is *major.* If the upper note has been lowered by a half-step the interval is *minor.* (The F is sharp in the key signature, so A to F♯ is a major sixth.) Therefore, A to F is a minor sixth.

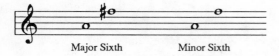

Major Sixth   Minor Sixth

Exercise 2

Identify the following Intervals. (See the example.)

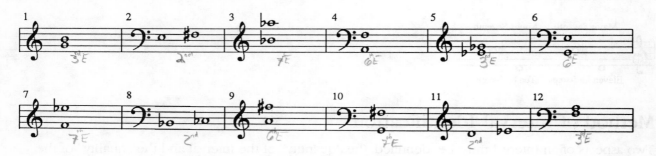

Perfect Intervals

In any major scale, the distance from the starting pitch to scale steps 1, 4, 5, and 8 is **perfect.** This term (in our present system) is used solely for the identification of intervals and is reserved only for those intervals whose frequency ratio is 1:1, 2:1, 3:2, or 4:3. (See chapter 1, Frequency.)
C Major Scale

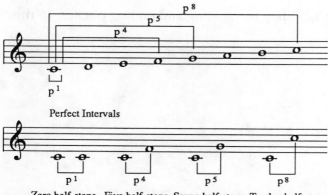

Perfect Intervals

Zero half-steps   Five half-steps   Seven half-steps   Twelve half-steps

F Major Scale

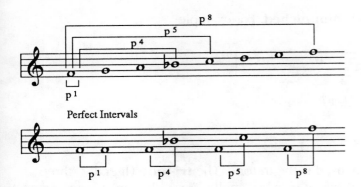

Perfect Intervals

Perfect 1 (perfect prime, perfect unison, or simply unison) has a frequency ratio of 1:1.
Perfect 8 (perfect octave) has a frequency ratio of 2:1. (This means that if a string vibrates at 440 vibrations per second, a string with the ratio 2:1 will vibrate at $2/1 \times 440$, or 880, vibrations per second—twice as fast.)
Perfect 5 (perfect fifth) has a frequency ratio of 3:2. (This means that if a string vibrates at 440 vibrations per second, a string with the ratio 3:2 will vibrate at $3/2 \times 440$, or 660, vibrations per second.)
Perfect 4 (perfect fourth) has a frequency ratio of 4:3. (This means that if a string vibrates at 440 vibrations per second, a string with the ratio 4:3 will vibrate at $4/3 \times 440$, or approximately 587, vibrations per second.)

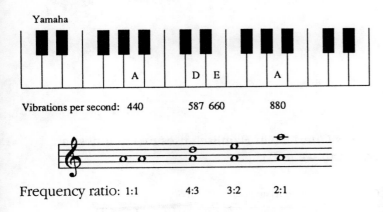

"Quality Adjustment" of Perfect Intervals

Augmented

Any perfect interval made larger by a half-step is **augmented.** For example:

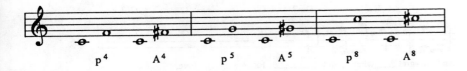

Diminished

Any perfect interval made smaller by a half-step is **diminished.** For example:

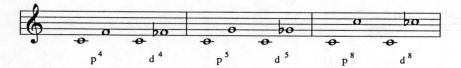

p⁴   d⁴   p⁵   d⁵   p⁸   d⁸

The Tri-Tone

Of these "adjusted" intervals the most commonly used is the tri-tone. The **tri-tone** (literally "three tones") is the distance of *three whole steps*. The distance may be "spelled" as either an augmented fourth or a diminished fifth. For example:

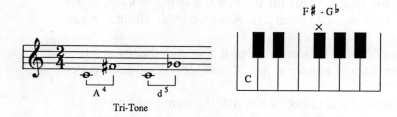

In the song "Do Re Mi" there is a tri-tone between measures 29 and 30. The distance from F to B is an augmented fourth:

In the song "What I Did for Love" from *Chorus Line,* Marvin Hamlisch uses two tri-tones (a diminished fifth—D to A♭—and an augmented fourth—F to B).

Exercise 3

Identify the following intervals. (Use the same method for interval identification outlined previously.) Intervals in this exercise will be either perfect, augmented, or diminished.

Problem: Identify the following interval.

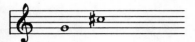

Solution:

1. Count the letter names between the notes. From G to C is a fourth.
2. Apply the major key signature of the bottom note.

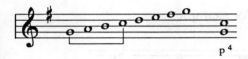

3. In the Key of G major, C is natural. Therefore, G to C is a perfect fourth. Since C is raised a half-step to C♯ in the example, the distance is made larger. The distance from G to C♯ is therefore an augmented fourth.

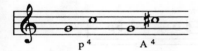

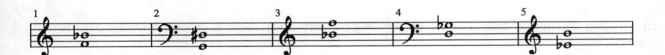

"Quality Adjustment" of Major-Minor Intervals

The quality adjustments of *augmented* and *diminished* can also be applied to major-minor Intervals. These intervals are possible in our musical system, but rare.

Augmented Intervals

Any major Interval made larger by a half-step is **augmented.** For example:

In the song "Michelle" by John Lennon and Paul McCartney there is an example of an augmented second:

Diminished Intervals

Any minor interval made smaller by a half-step is diminished. For example:

A major interval is diminished by making it smaller by two half-steps (one whole step). For example:

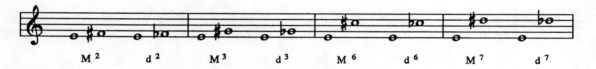

In the song "Anatevka" from *Fiddler on the Roof* by Jerry Bock, there is an example of a diminished seventh:

*See "Pythagorean Theorem Applied to Intervals" at the end of this chapter.

Exercise 4

Identify the following intervals. (Use the same method for interval identification outlined previously.) Intervals in this exercise will be major, minor, augmented, or diminished.
Problem: Identify the following interval.

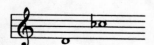

Solution:

1. Count: D to C is a seventh
2. Apply the major key signature of the bottom note.

3. In the key of D Major, C is sharp. The distance from D to C♯ is therefore a major seventh. The distance from D to C is a minor seventh, and the interval from D to C♭ is a diminished seventh.

Identifying Intervals in a Song

We can now use this information to identify the melodic intervals in a song. When identifying melodic intervals, always identify the distance between successive pitches by using the key signature of the *lowest sounding pitch*. (It doesn't matter whether the lowest pitch is the first or second tone. The distance between them is the same.)

Here are the intervals between each tone of the song "Do Re Mi." Arrows indicate the direction of the melodic interval (up or down).

Example:

Do Re Mi (Measures 1-8)

Do Re Mi (Measures 13-20)

Exercise 5

Identify *all* of the melodic intervals in the following songs. Indicate the direction of the interval by an arrow (up or down—see the example of "Do Re Mi"). Sing each song, listening to the intervals. These examples contain only major, minor, and perfect intervals.

Younger Than Springtime (R. Rodgers: South Pacific)

Comedy Tonight (S. Sondheim: A Funny Thing Happened on the Way to the Forum)

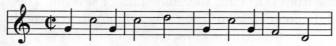

Old Folks at Home (S. Foster)

All of the examples in exercise 5 were in the key of C major. When identifying the intervals of a melody in any other key, it is necessary to remember how the key signature affects every pitch. Before identifying the interval write the exact pitch of each note below the note. For example:

Shenandoah (traditional)

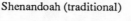

Exercise 6

In each of the following songs identify every pitch according to the accidentals in the key signature. Then identify all of the melodic intervals and indicate the direction of the interval by an arrow. Sing each song, listening to the interval. (See the example of "Shenandoah".) These examples contain only major, minor, and perfect intervals.

Home on the Range (D. Kelley and B. Higley)

Hey Jude (J. Lennon and P. McCartney)

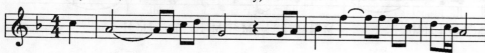

Somewhere Over the Rainbow (H. Arlen: <u>The Wizard of Oz</u>)

Exercise 7

Identify all the intervals within each set of brackets. (First identify every pitch according to the accidentals in the key signature.) These examples contain major, minor, perfect, and augmented intervals.

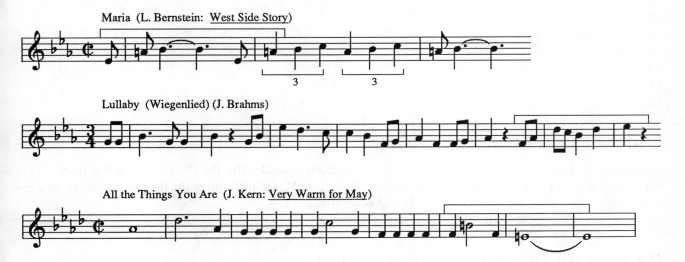

Maria (L. Bernstein: <u>West Side Story</u>)

Lullaby (Wiegenlied) (J. Brahms)

All the Things You Are (J. Kern: <u>Very Warm for May</u>)

Consonance and Dissonance

Intervals can be classified as either **consonant** or **dissonant**. This classification is subjective not only for individuals but for entire periods of music history. In some eras certain intervals which are now considered consonant were thought to be dissonant. (In the thirteenth century, for example, major and minor thirds were "imperfect" and major and minor sixths were dissonant. Today these intervals are considered consonant.)

Sometimes intervals are referred to as **active** (dissonant) or **inactive** (consonant), but this still leaves room for subjectivity. No definition seems to be totally satisfactory.

Exercise 8

Instructor: Play all of the listed intervals in any order. (Play each interval twice.)
Students: Identify each interval as C (consonant), D (dissonant) or ? (cannot decide).
Instructor: Survey the class. Which intervals did the majority of the class agree on? Which did they disagree on? Did students identify any interval the same way twice? (If numbers 1 and 18 were perfect fourths, how many students had the same response for both?)
Intervals

	P4	m7
m2	P5	M7
M2	Tri-tone	P8
m3	m6	
M3	M6	

Use the following lists of definitions to help you classify the intervals.

Consonant In agreement, harmonious, in a state of rest, pleasing	Dissonant Disagreeable, inharmonious, in a state of unrest, harsh, unpleasant
1.	13.
2.	14.
3.	15.
4.	16.
5.	17.
6.	18.
7.	19.
8.	20.
9.	21.
10.	22.
11.	23.
12.	24.

Order of Consonance

Following are two lists for the order of consonance. Both consider the P8, P5, and P4 as the most consonant intervals and the tri-tone as the most dissonant. Major and minor thirds and sixths are more consonant than major and minor seconds and sevenths.

Compare your survey with the two lists that follow.

Pythagorean Theory (Ratio of Frequencies)

P8   P5   P4   M6   M3   m3   m6   M2   M7   m2   m7   Tri-tone
This theory holds that the smaller the frequency ratio, the more **consonant** the sound. Frequency ratios for perfect intervals are as follows: P8 (2:1), P5 (3:2), and P4 (4:3). Compare these to the frequency ratio of the tri-tone: 729:512.

Paul Hindemith (Twentieth-Century Composer-Theorist): <u>The Craft of Musical Composition</u>

P8   P5   P4   M3   m6   m3   M6   M2   m7   m2   M7   Tri-tone

Compound Intervals

Compound intervals are intervals that are greater than an octave. Between measures 12 and 13 of the song "Greensleeves" you will see a compound interval:

To compute a compound interval, use the following process:

1. Reduce the interval by writing the upper note an octave lower.

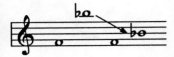

2. Identify the *new* distance (1. count; 2. apply a major key signature; 3. compare).

3. Add 7 to the distance you computed in step 2. (The *quality* of the interval does *not* change.)

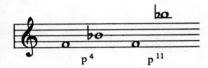

If we reduce the compound interval in the song "Greensleeves" and compute the distance, we find that the distance from B to D is a minor third (three letter names and three half-steps).

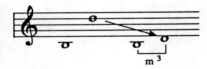

The original distance is therefore a minor tenth.

Exercise 9

Identify the following compound intervals.

Exercise 10

In the following pieces compound intervals appear in brackets (⌐¬). Identify each interval according to the process just outlined. (Remember to identify pitches according to the accidentals in the key signature.)

The Star Spangled Banner (traditional melody)

Come Scoglio (W. A. Mozart: Cosi Fan Tutte)

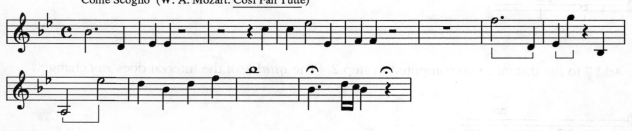

Bess, You Is My Woman Now (G. Gershwin: Porgy and Bess)

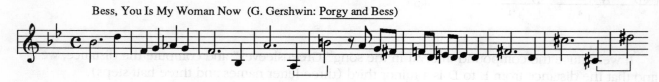

Additional Exercises

Sight Singing Exercises

Exercise 1

Sing a major scale; then sing the following intervals.

Keyboard Exercises

Exercise 1

Play the following examples; first with the right hand alone, then the left hand alone, then with both hands together. *Sing* the interval the *second* time you play it. (This exercise is designed not only as interval practice but also as a hand-stretching exercise.)

Other Concepts and Exercises

Interval Quantity: Observation

When placed on the staff, if both notes are on lines or both are on spaces, the interval will be an odd number regardless of the clef. For example:

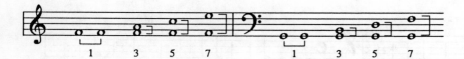

If one note is on a line and the other note is on a space, the interval will be an even number regardless of clef. For example:

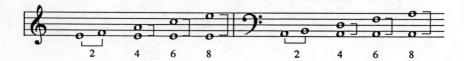

These statements are also true even if one note is in the treble clef and the other note is in the bass clef:

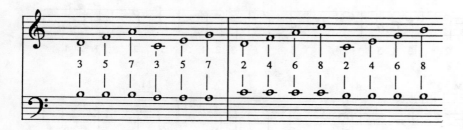

Exercise 1

Identify the following interval quantities. No clefs are given in this exercise because the *quantity* of an interval is not affected by the clef.

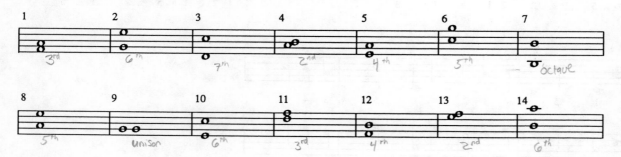

Writing Intervals

Apply the same procedure for writing intervals as you did for identifying them.

Problem: Write a pitch a minor sixth above F.

Solution:

1. Count: From F up six letter names is D.

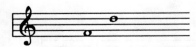

2. Apply a key signature: The key signature for F major is one flat (B). The sixth scale step (D) is natural in the scale. The distance from F to D is therefore a Major sixth.

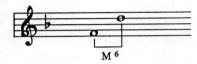

3. Adjust (compare): To make a major distance minor, lower the upper note a half-step by adding an accidental.

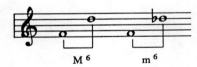

(Note: Never make an enharmonic adjustment [D♭ = C♯] since this will alter the *quantity* of the interval. The distance from F to D♭ is a *minor sixth,* while the distance from F to C♯ is an *augmented fifth.*)

Exercise 2

Write the following intervals *above* the given pitches. enharmonic

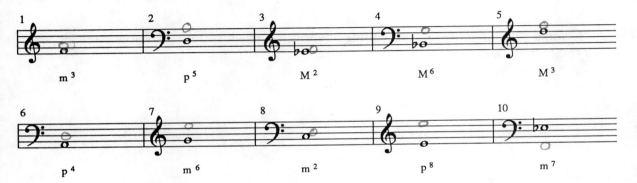

One of the purposes of intervals is to aid students and musicians in sight-singing music. Many musicians memorize the sound of an interval by relating it to the first two notes of a song. For example, "My Bonnie Lies Over the Ocean" begins with a major sixth.

Exercise 3

Your instructor will play the following intervals. Name songs that begin with that interval. (With some intervals you will find many songs, while with others you may have difficulty finding one. Discuss the results.)

Pythagorean Theorem Applied to Intervals

Pythagoras, a Greek scholar of the sixth century B.C., developed the following mathematical formula: $A^2 + B^2 = C^2$. The corollary to this formula is $1 + A^2 + B^2 = C^2 + 1$. (If you add one to both sides of an equation you do not change the equation.)

Let's use the concept of this corollary formula to compute intervals. On the keyboard the pitches A and E are seven half-steps apart (a perfect fifth).

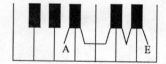   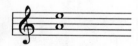

If we raise A up a half-step to A♯ and E up a half-step to E♯, we have *not* altered the distance *between* the two pitches.

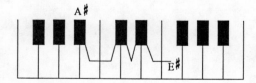   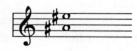

Use this formula when identifying (or writing) intervals for which you do not know a key signature for the bottom note.

Problem: Identify the following interval.

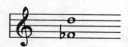

Solution:

1. Since there is no practical key signature for F♭ major, raise the bottom note up a half-step to the pitch F.

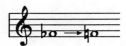

2. To keep the distance *between* the pitches the same, change the upper note of the interval in the *same direction*.

Again, alterations are made only with accidentals. Never change letter names since this would change the quantity of the interval.

The distance between these two new pitches will be exactly the same as the distance between the two original pitches.

Exercise 4

Each of the following intervals has a bottom note that does not have a practical major key signature. Change both notes in the *same direction* to identify the interval.

Exercise 5

Identify all of the melodic intervals marked by brackets in the following songs.

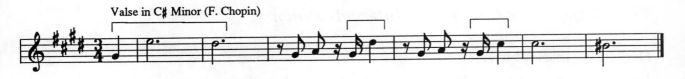

Valse in C♯ Minor (F. Chopin)

Fugue No. 24 in B Minor (J. S. Bach: Well Tempered Clavier Book I)

My Favorite Things (R. Rodgers: The Sound of Music)

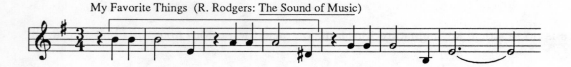

Double Accidentals

In some cases it is necessary to use a double accidental when making an adjustment to major or perfect intervals.
Examples:

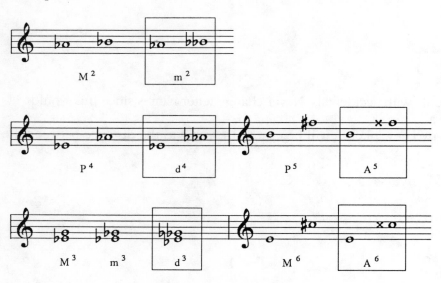

Exercise 6

Write the following intervals above the given pitches.

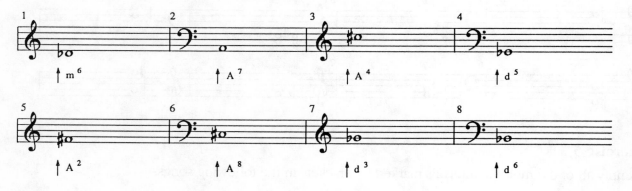

Two Methods for Computing Intervals Down

Method 1 (Interval Inversion)

Inversion means to turn upside down or reverse position. Inverting an interval puts the top note on the bottom or the bottom note on top. For example:

Let's think in mathematical terms. A foot-long ruler has twelve inches. If we measure eight inches there will be four inches remaining.

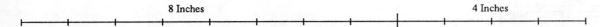

On the piano keyboard there are twelve half-steps in an octave. If we measure eight half-steps (a minor sixth), there will be four half-steps remaining (a major third).

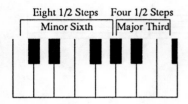

Formula for Interval Inversion

Major intervals invert to minor. Minor intervals invert to major. (See the example of an inverted interval.)

Augmented intervals invert to diminished. Diminished intervals invert to augmented.

Perfect intervals remain perfect. (Only the numbers change.)

The numbers in an inversion add up to nine. (A fifth becomes a fourth, a third becomes a sixth, and so on.)

Formula: P ◄──► P   **Numbers add up to nine**
           M ◄──► m
           A ◄──► d

Exercise 7A

Write each of the following intervals *below* the given pitch using interval inversion.
Problem: What note is a major sixth *below* F?

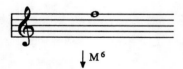

Solution:

1. Invert the interval (the problem): What note is a minor third *above* F?

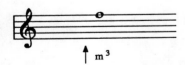

2. Work this as a regular problem.

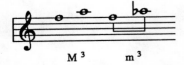

3. Invert the answer. (Put the upper note on the bottom.)

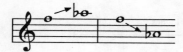

From F up a minor third is A♭; therefore, from F down a major sixth is also A♭.

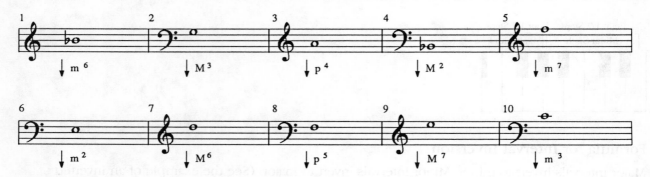

Method 2 (Adjusting the Lowest Tone)

Use the same process that you use to compute a normal interval; however, in making alterations, change the *bottom note* as follows:

1. When you would normally lower the upper note to make a distance smaller, *raise the bottom note instead.*
2. When you would normally raise the upper note to make a distance larger; *lower the bottom note instead.*

Exercise 7B

Write each of the following intervals *below* the given pitch.
Problem: What note is a major sixth *below* C?

Solution:

1. Count: C down six letter names is E.

2. Apply the key signature of the bottom note (E).

In the key of E major, C is sharp. From E to C♯ is a major sixth. From E to C is a minor sixth.

F[C]G D   M⁶   m⁶

3. Adjust: To make this interval major (a half-step larger than minor), *lower the bottom note.*

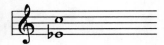

From E♭ to C is a major sixth.
Check: In the key of E♭ major, C is natural. From E♭ to C is, therefore, a major sixth.

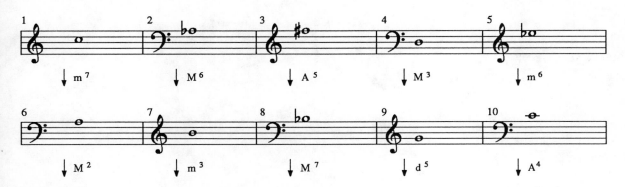

Chapter **10** *Chords*

Music is composed of three elements: rhythm (meter), melody, and harmony.

Let's return to the song "Do Re Mi."

In the uppermost treble clef we find the **melody** (the "horizontal" structure of a composition). The lower two clefs (treble and bass) contain both the melody and the **harmony** (the "vertical" structure of a composition). Harmony is the simultaneous sounding of pitches called **chords.** (The term "harmony" means "in agreement" or "the pleasing arrangement of parts.")

Chords generally consist of three or more tones played together. When only two tones sound simultaneously, we usually refer to the sound as a **harmonic interval** (see chapter 9). A chord may be any combination of tones.

Instructor: Play the following examples.

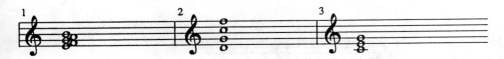

Chords are generally classified according to specific characteristics. We will limit our discussion to one classification (the one most frequently used since the mid-seventeenth century): the **triad** (chord 3 in the example).

Triads

A triad is a chord that contains *three* tones, each a *third apart*.

Say the letters of the musical alphabet in thirds (read the underlined letters below):

A B C D E F G A B C D E F G A

By saying any three consecutive underlined letters, you can "spell" *any* triad. For example:

On the staff, consecutive thirds are written either all on lines or all on spaces. For example:

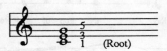

The tones of a triad are numbered from the bottom upward: 1, 3, 5. The first tone (1) is usually referred to as the **root.** This tone gives us the name of the triad. For example:

(C is the root of the triad.)

Exercise 1

Build a triad on each of the given pitches (one in the treble and one in the bass clef). Identify the root of each triad.

Types of Triads

There are *four* types of traids: major, minor, augmented, and diminished. The last two (augmented and diminished) will be discussed later in this chapter. First let's concentrate on the two most commonly used triads: major and minor.

Identifying and Writing Triads

Major Triads

A major triad consists of the first, third, and fifth scale steps of a major scale. For example:

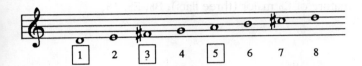

In its simplest form (all three tones on consecutive lines or spaces), the upper two tones (the third and fifth) will "fit" in the key signature of the lowest tone. For example:

In the key of D major, F and C are both sharp.

In the D major triad, F is sharp and A is natural. (There is no C in the triad.)

Intervallic Relationship: In a major triad the distance between the root and the third is a *major* third. The distance between the third and the fifth is a *minor* third. For example:

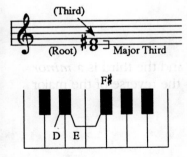

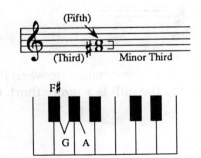

Exercise 2

Make the following triads major by adding accidentals (wherever necessary) to the upper two notes, making them fit into the scale of the lowest sounding tone.
Example: Make the following triad major.

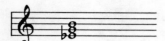

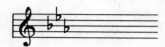

1. Write the key signature of E♭ major (three flats): B♭, E♭, A♭.

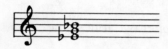

2. In the E♭ major triad, the upper two tones are G and B. In the key of E♭ major, G is natural and B is flat.

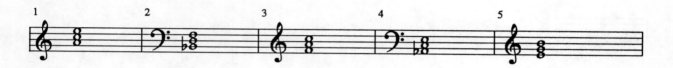

Minor Triads

The minor triad is derived from the major triad by making the following adjustment:
Lower the third of a *major triad* by a half-step. (The third of a triad refers to the middle pitch: 1 **3** 5. This is the third tone of the scale.)
Example:

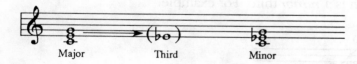

Intervallic Relationship: In a minor triad the distance between the root and the third is a *minor* third. The distance between the third and the fifth is a *major* third. (This is the reverse of the major triad.)
Example:

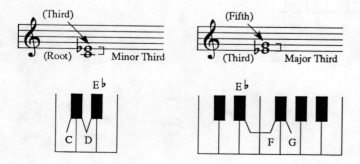

Exercise 3

Make each of the following traids major, then lower the third of the major triad by a half-step to make it minor.

Example: Make the following triad minor.

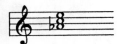

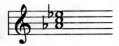

1. First make the triad major. (In the key of A♭ major, C is natural and E is flat.)

2. Lower the third of this major triad by a half-step to make a minor triad. (C is lowered to C♭.)

Exercise 4

Identify the following triads. Identify the letter name of the triad (the root) and the type of triad (major or minor).

Example: Identify the following triad.

1. This is an F triad because the lowest sounding tone in its simplest form is F.

2. In the major key of F, the B is flat. The notes A and C are natural.

3. Since the third of the triad (A) has been lowered by a half-step, the type of triad is minor.

Exercise 5

Write the following triads.
Example: Write a D minor triad.

1. Write a chord in thirds beginning on D.

2. Apply the key signature of the bottom note to make a major triad.

D Major

3. Adjust to make the triad minor: lower the third of the major triad by a half-step.

D Minor

1	2	3	4
E♭ Major	B♭ Minor	D Major	A Minor
5	6	7	8
E Minor	F Major	E♭ Minor	A♭ Minor

Naming System

Chord symbols (letters and numbers) are a musical shorthand usually placed above a melody. Letters indicate the type of triad, while numbers indicate added tones. (Numbers will be discussed in the next chapter.) Example:

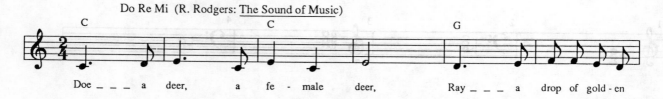

Do Re Mi (R. Rodgers: The Sound of Music)

Doe _ _ _ a deer, a fe - male deer, Ray _ _ _ a drop of gold - en

A letter name indicates a major triad unless followed by a lower case *m*. The lowercase m indicates a minor triad:

Major Triads   **Minor Triads**

D   Dm
Bb   Bbm
F   Fm

A triad sounds until another chord symbol is written. The chord may be held or restruck. For example:

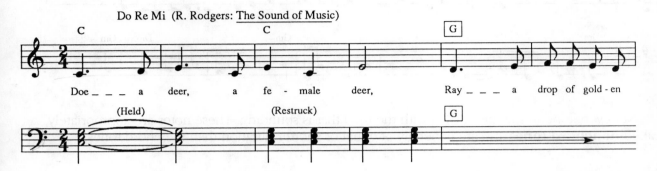

The rhythm of a chord is indicated by the placement of the chord symbol. Each chord is written over the melody *exactly* where it should sound.

Example:

In the song "America," the C chord in measure 3 sounds for *two* beats. The F chord sounds *on the third beat* and lasts only *one* beat.

Exercise 6

In each of the following songs identify each chord as major or minor. Above each chord write the number of beats the chord sounds.

Edelweiss (R. Rodgers: The Sound of Music)

A Time For Us (N. Rota: Romeo and Juliet)

Not every tone in the melody fits with the triad that is sounding. These notes are appropriately called **nonchord tones** and are generally of equal or shorter duration than the chord tones.

Exercise 7

In exercise 6 circle all nonchord tones.

Augmented and Diminished Triads

The remaining two types of triads are augmented and diminished. These triads are less frequently used than major and minor triads.

Augmented Triads

An augmented triad is derived from the major triad by making the following adjustment: *Raise* the fifth of a *major triad* by a half-step. (Adjustments are made only with accidentals; never change letter names.) For example:

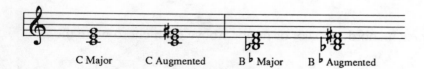

C Major   C Augmented   B♭ Major   B♭ Augmented

(Augmented chords may contain *both* sharps and flats.)
Intervallic Relationship: An augmented triad consists of *two consecutive major thirds.* For example:

Major Third   Major Third

The distance between the root and the fifth of the triad is an augmented fifth:

Exercise 8

Write the following augmented triads.

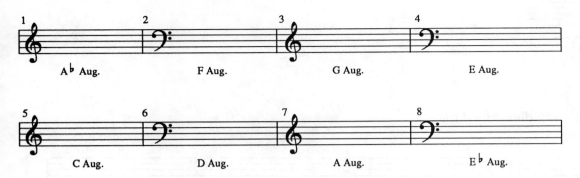

A♭ Aug.   F Aug.   G Aug.   E Aug.

C Aug.   D Aug.   A Aug.   E♭ Aug.

A plus sign (+) placed after a chord (D+, B♭+) indicates that a triad is augmented. Sometimes composers abbreviate the word: D Aug., B♭ Aug. For example:

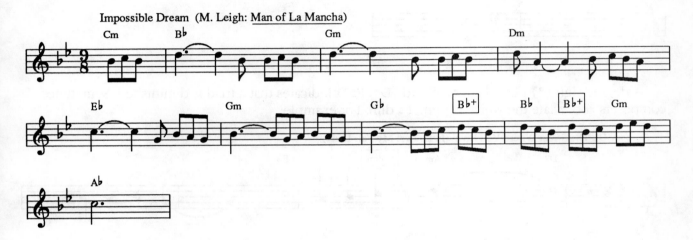

Impossible Dream (M. Leigh: Man of La Mancha)

Diminished Triads

A diminished triad is derived from the major triad by making the following adjustment: *Lower* the third *and* fifth of a *major triad* by a half-step. (Adjustments are made only with accidentals; never change letter names.)
Example:

C Major   C Diminished   A Major   A Diminished

Intervallic Relationship: A diminished triad consists of *two consecutive minor thirds.* For example:

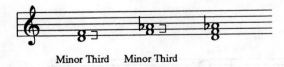

Minor Third   Minor Third

The distance between the root and the fifth of the triad is a diminished fifth:

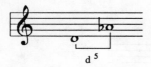

Exercise 9

Write the following diminished triads.

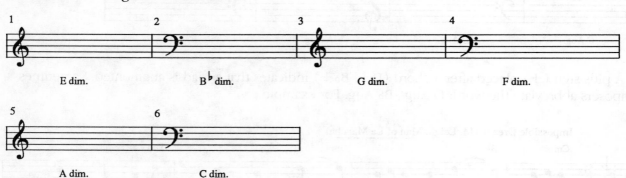

1   E dim.
2   B♭ dim.
3   G dim.
4   F dim.
5   A dim.
6   C dim.

A degree sign (°) placed after a chord (D°, F♯°) indicates that a triad is diminished. Sometimes composers abbreviate the word: D dim., F♯ dim. For example:

On The Street Where You Live (F. Loewe: My Fair Lady)

Exercise 10

Identify the following triads: major, minor, augmented, or diminished.

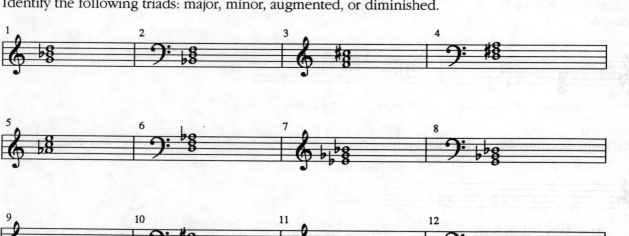

Identification of Chords in a Key

Now that we have an understanding of the four types of triads, we should be able to identify triads in a key (major or minor). This identification shows the *relationship* of the triads in a key to the tonic.

Relationship of Triads in Any Major Key

If we build a triad on each tone of a major scale using only the tones that appear in that scale, we will discover the following pattern:

M m m M M m d M
(M = Major, m = minor, and d = diminished)

Example: D Major

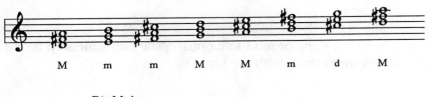

M   m   m   M   M   m   d   M

Bb Major

M   m   m   M   M   m   d   M

Using a capital Roman numeral for major chords and a small Roman numeral for minor chords, we arrive at the following formula for triads as they appear in every major scale:

I ii iii IV V vi vii° I

The diminished triad is written with a *small* Roman numeral and a degree sign.

Observations

Three triads are major: I   IV   and V
Three triads are minor: ii   iii   and vi
One triad is diminished: vii°
There are no augmented triads.

In chapter 5 we learned that every scale step has a name. This name is also used to identify the *triad* built on that scale step.

I   Tonic (tone): The beginning pitch of the scale.

ii   Supertonic (super: above, tonic: tone): The tone above the tonic.

iii Mediant (middle): The tone between the tonic and the dominant.

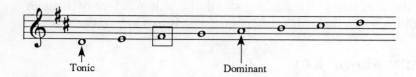

IV Subdominant (sub: below): The tone a perfect fifth below the upper tonic.

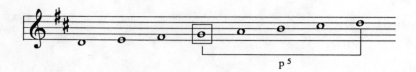

V Dominant: The tone a perfect fifth above the tonic.

(The word "dominant" literally means "controlling or most influential." The fifth scale step is one of the dominating tones of the scale, sharing importance with the tonic.)

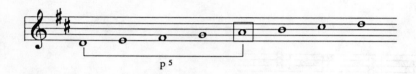

vi Submediant (sub: below, mediant: middle): The tone between the subdominant and the upper tonic.

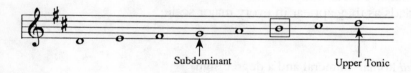

vii° Leading Tone: The tone that leads to the tonic.

Exercise 11

Complete the following chart.

Key:	I	ii	iii	IV	V	vi	vii°
D Major	D	Em	F#m	G	A	Bm	C# dim.
F Major	F			Bb	C		E dim.
G Major		Am	Bm			Em	F# dim.
Bb Major					F	Gm	
A Major	A	Bm	C#m				G# dim.
Eb Major							

Exercise 12

Identify every chord in the following songs by their tonal relationship (Roman numerals). Refer to the chart in exercise 11.

Example:

Key: C Major:

I	ii	iii	IV	V	vi	vii°
C	Dm	Em	F	G	Am	B dim.

Chord progression (Order of chords in the song)

	C	Am	F	Em	Dm	Am	G	C
Tonal relationship:	I	vi	IV	iii	ii	vi	V	I

Relationship of Triads in the Harmonic Minor

The harmonic minor is used to harmonize a song written in a minor key. The harmonic minor scale is the same as the natural minor with the exception of a **raised** seventh scale step.
Example: D Natural Minor (Same key signature as F major)

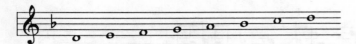

D Harmonic Minor

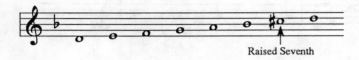

Raised Seventh

This seventh step **melodically** pulls to the tonic. **Harmonically,** this scale step appears in the dominant triad (as the third of the chord), making it major. The major dominant triad has a strong pull to the tonic triad. This *pull to the tonic* is the reason for the harmonic minor. Example:

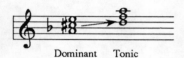

Dominant   Tonic

If we build a triad on each tone of a harmonic minor scale using only tones that appear in that scale, the following pattern emerges:

m   d   A+   m   M   M   d

(M = Major, m = minor, A = Augmented, d = diminished)

Using Roman numerals, we arrive at the following formula for triads as they appear in the harmonic minor:

i   ii°   III+   iv   V   VI   vii°   i

(The augmented triad is written with a *large* Roman numeral and a plus sign to the upper right.)

Observations

Two triads are minor: i and iv
Two triads are major: V and VI
Two triads are diminished: ii° and vii°
One triad is augmented: III+

Exercise 13

Complete the following chart for the harmonic minor.

	i	ii°	III+	iv	V	VI	vii°
Key: D Minor	Dm	E dim.	F Aug.	Gm	A	Bb	C♯ dim.
G Minor	Gm		Bb Aug.	Cm			
A Minor				Dm	F		G♯ dim.
E Minor			G Aug.		B	C	
C Minor							

Exercise 14

Identify every chord in the following songs by their tonal relationships (Roman numerals). Each piece is in the harmonic minor. Refer to the chart in exercise 13.
Example:

Love Theme (N. Rota: The Godfather)

Key: C Minor (See chart in exercise 13)

Chord Progression:	Cm	Fm	Cm	Fm	Cm	G	Cm
Tonal Relationship:	i	iv	i	iv	i	V	i

1.

My Funny Valentine (R. Rodgers: Babes in Arms)

Sometimes I Feel Like a Motherless Child (spiritual)

Additional Exercises

Sight Singing Exercises

Exercise 1

Sing the following triads. Use a neutral "ah" vowel. Repeat this exercise beginning on F, Bb, G, and D.

Instructor: Play the triads as students sing.

Keyboard Exercises

Exercise 1

Play the following triads, first with the right hand, then with the left. Repeat the pattern beginning on F, Bb, G, and D.

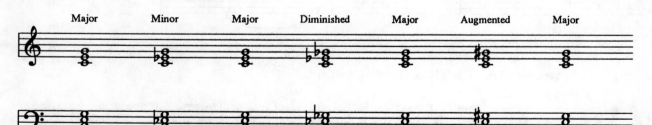

Exercise 2

Play the following primary triads (tonic, subdominant, and dominant) in each of the following keys.
Major Keys

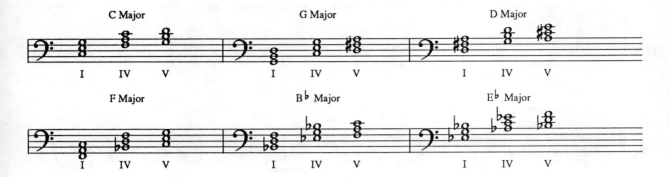

Minor Keys

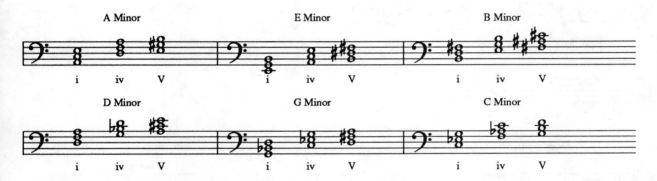

Exercise 3

The following songs can be harmonized using only these primary chords. Remember, not every tone in the melody fits into the chord that is sounding at the same time.

Instructor: Ask a member of the class to play the chords while the rest of the class sings the melody.

Variations on Exercise 3:
1. Ask two students to play the song on the piano; one student should play the melody while the other plays the chords.
2. Ask two students to play the song; one student should play the melody on an instrument other than the piano while the second student plays the chords on the piano.
3. Those students who have had enough piano experience should try playing the entire song, both melody and chords.

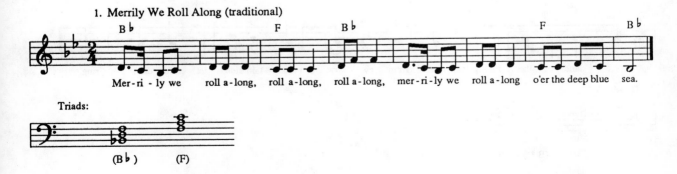

2. Row, Row, Row Your Boat (traditional)

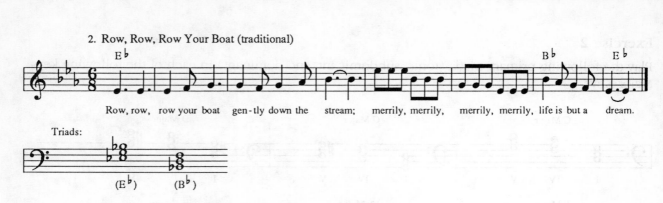

Row, row, row your boat gen-tly down the stream; merrily, merrily, merrily, merrily, life is but a dream.

Triads:

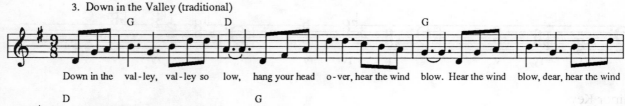

(E♭)   (B♭)

3. Down in the Valley (traditional)

Down in the val-ley, val-ley so low, hang your head o-ver, hear the wind blow. Hear the wind blow, dear, hear the wind

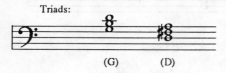

blow, hang your head o-ver hear the wind blow.

Triads:

(G)   (D)

4. Goodnight, Ladies (E. Christy)

Good-night, la-dies; good-night, la-dies; good-night, la-dies; we're going to leave you now.

Triads:

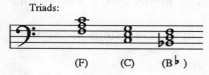

(F)   (C)   (B♭)

5. America (My Country 'tis of Thee) (traditional melody)

My coun-try, 'tis of thee, sweet land of li-ber-ty, of thee I sing. Land where my fa-thers died,

land of the Pil-grims' pride, from ev-'ry moun-tain side, let free-dom ring.

Triads:

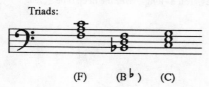

(F)   (B♭)   (C)

Other Concepts and Exercises

Augmented and Diminished Triads Requiring Double Accidentals

It is sometimes necessary to use a double sharp (**×**) to make a chord augmented.
Example:

B Major   B Augmented

Likewise, there are times when it is necessary to use a double flat (♭♭) in order to make a chord diminished.
Example:

E♭ Major   E♭ Diminished

Exercise 1

Write the following augmented and diminished chords. Double accidentals are *not* necessary in every example in this exercise.

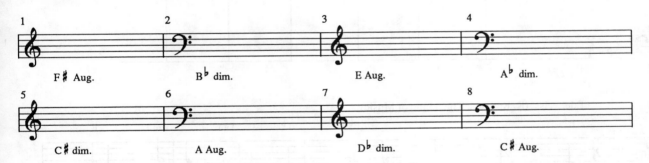

1 F♯ Aug.   2 B♭ dim.   3 E Aug.   4 A♭ dim.

5 C♯ dim.   6 A Aug.   7 D♭ dim.   8 C♯ Aug.

Exercise 2

The following melodies are written with chord symbols. Since chords are generally played *below* a melody (on a lower pitch), write each of the triads in the bass clef. Notate the rhythm of each chord.
Example:

America (My Country 'tis of Thee) (traditional)
C   G   C   F   C   G   C

In measures 2 and 5, the G chord could have been written as follows:

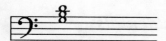

It is written down an octave so as not to interfere with the tones of the melody. **In this exercise the octave placement of the chords is unimportant.** Although certain theoretical rules are being broken in this example, at this stage it is more important to have some practical application of harmonization than to concern ourselves with complex rules.

Goodnight, Ladies (E. Christy)

Joy to the World (G. F. Handel)

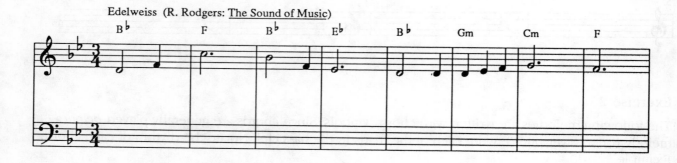

Edelweiss (R. Rodgers: The Sound of Music)

Chapter 11 Seventh Chords and Chord Inversions

In chapter 10, we discussed the fact that chord symbols are a musical shorthand using letters *and numbers.*
Example:

Do Re Mi (R. Rodgers: The Sound of Music)

The most frequently added tone is the seventh. When a triad contains a seventh it is referred to as a seventh chord.

Dominant Seventh Chords

Although many possibilities exist when dealing with adding sevenths to chords, we will limit our discussion to one: the addition of a minor seventh to the *dominant* triad. (V⁷)
Example: Key of C

The addition of this tone creates the distance of a tri-tone with the third of the chord.
Example:

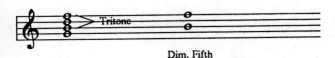

In chapter 9 we discovered that the interval of the tri-tone is the most *dissonant* of all the intervals. The dominant seventh chord, therefore, becomes an active chord that wants to resolve (settle). This chord generally resolves to the tonic (starting tone of the scale). For example:

la - ti - do!

C: V⁷   I

Exercise 1

Write the dominant triad in each of the following keys. Add a minor seventh from the root of the triad to make a dominant seventh chord.

1 G Major 2 B♭ Major 3 F Major 4 A Major

5 D Major V⁷ 6 E♭ Major V⁷ 7 A♭ Major V⁷ 8 E Major V⁷

Exercise 2

The following melodies are written with chord symbols and include dominant seventh chords. In each example triads sound for either one or two measures. Write each triad in the bass clef provided with appropriate rhythm.
Example:

Camptown Races (S. Foster)

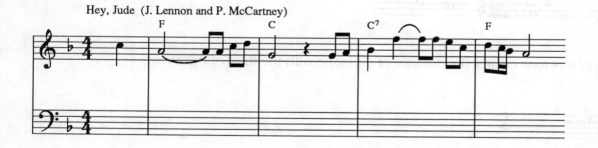

Hey, Jude (J. Lennon and P. McCartney)

Silver Bells (J. Livingston and R. Evans)

More (R. Ortolani and N. Oliviero) (Theme from <u>Mondo Cane</u>)

Chord Inversions

The term **inversion** means to turn upside down or reverse position. Inverting a triad changes the position of the tones *without changing the name or type of triad.*

Root Position

A triad is in root position if the root of the triad is the lowest sounding tone. For example:

First Inversion

A triad is in first inversion if the third of the triad is the lowest sounding tone. For example:

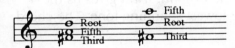

In this example, the root of the chord (D) had been inverted and placed elsewhere in the triad (not necessarily on top, but *above* the third).

Second Inversion

A triad is in second inversion if the fifth of the triad is the lowest sounding tone. For example:

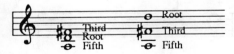

In this example, both the root and the third have been inverted and placed above the fifth.

Identifying Triads that Are Not in Their Simplest Forms

To identify a triad that is not in its simplest form (with all notes on consecutive lines or spaces), take the following three steps.
Example: Identify the following triad.

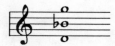

1. *Arrange the tones on the staff in thirds* (all on consecutive lines or spaces). (It does not matter in which octave the notes are placed.)

As an alternative, arrange the letter names so that they are each three letter names apart. For example; in the original example the letter names from bottom to top are: D   B   G
These tones arranged in thirds are: <u>G</u>   A   <u>B</u>   C   <u>D</u>
Step 1 puts the triad in its *simplest form*. The *lowest* tone gives us the name of the triad.

2. *Identify the type of triad.* To do so, apply the major key signature: In the key of G major, both B and D are natural. Since the third (B) is lowered by a half-step in the example, the triad is minor. *Intervallic relationship:* G to B♭ is a minor third (three half-steps) and B♭ to D is a major third (four half-steps). The triad is therefore minor.

3. *Identify the inversion.* The lowest sounding (written) tone in the *original triad* gives us the inversion. In the example, the D (the fifth of the chord) is the lowest sounding tone. The chord is therefore in second inversion.

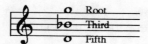

Exercise 3

Identify the following types of triads and their inversions.

Inversions of the Dominant Seventh Chord

Since the dominant seventh chord (V⁷) has an additional tone (the seventh) it also has an additional inversion.

Third Inversion

A dominant seventh chord is in third Inversion if the seventh is the lowest sounding tone. For example:

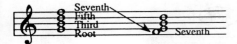

Exercise 4

Identify the following dominant seventh chords and their inversions.

The Purpose of Chord Inversions

There are two main reasons for using chord inversions:

1. One of the most important reasons for chord inversion is to create a smooth connection between triads. For example:

Chord symbols only indicate the *tones* of a triad. The *order* of those tones (inversion) is generally *not* specified but is left up to the performer. When an inversion is desired the following notation is used:

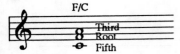

The first letter indicates the **chord** while the second letter indicates the **lowest sounding tone.** In this example, the lowest sounding tone (C) is the fifth of the triad, making it a second inversion chord.

2. A second reason for chord inversion is to weaken a chord and create an "unsettled" or "suspended" feeling. (For this reason an inversion is not commonly used as the final chord of a song.)

Exercise 5

In the following songs, circle all chords that are inverted. Identify the chord (by *letter name* and *type of triad*). Write the triad and name the inversion.

Example:

America (My Country 'tis of Thee) (traditional)

G Major
(2nd Inversion)

A Major
(with a Minor 7th)
(1st Inversion)

A Major
(1st Inversion)

Sicilian Hymn (XVIII Century)

Yesterday (J. Lennon and P. McCartney)

How Lovely Is Thy Dwelling Place (J. Brahms: Requiem)

Notating Inversions when Using Roman Numerals

Basic Triads (Triads containing only a root, third, and fifth)

Root Position (The root of the triad is the lowest sounding tone)

Using *only* the Roman numeral indicates *root position*. For example:

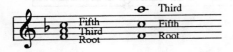

First Inversion (The third of the triad is the lowest sounding tone)

The numbers $^6_3$ (some theorists only use 6) placed after a Roman numeral indicate first inversion.

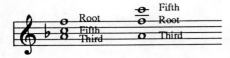

The numbers 6 and 3 indicate the letter names (not necessarily the placement) of the other two pitches of the chord. For example:

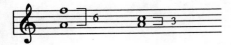

Six letter names above A is F and three letter names above A is C.

Second Inversion (The fifth of the triad is the lowest sounding tone)

The numbers $\begin{smallmatrix}6\\4\end{smallmatrix}$ placed after a Roman numeral indicate second inversion.

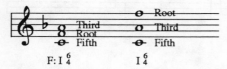

The numbers 6 and 4 indicate the letter names (not necessarily the placement) of the other two pitches of the chord. For example:

Six letter names above C is A, and four letter names above C is F.

Exercise 6

Identify the following chords in the given major and minor keys, using Roman numerals. Indicate the correct inversion by the use of the numbers 6 and $\begin{smallmatrix}6\\4\end{smallmatrix}$.

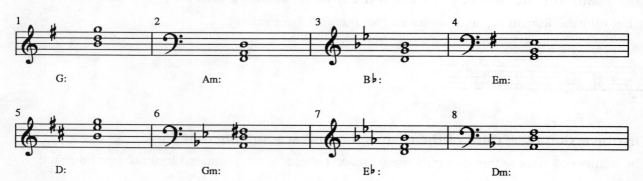

Dominant Seventh Chords (Inversions)

Root Position (The root of the triad is the lowest sounding tone)

The number 7 placed after the Roman numeral indicates root position. For example:

First Inversion (The third of the triad is the lowest sounding tone)

The numbers $\begin{smallmatrix}6\\5\\3\end{smallmatrix}$ (usually only $\begin{smallmatrix}6\\5\end{smallmatrix}$) placed after a Roman numeral indicate first inverison. The numbers 6, 5, and 3 indicate the letter names (not necessarily the placement) of the root, seventh, and fifth, respectively. For example:

Second Inversion (The fifth of the triad is the lowest sounding tone)

The numbers $\frac{6}{4}$ (usually $\frac{4}{3}$) placed after a Roman numeral indicate second inversion. The numbers 6, 4, and 3 indicate the letter names (not necessarily the placement) of the third, root, and seventh, respectively. For example:

G: V$\frac{4}{3}$

Third Inversion (The seventh of the triad is the lowest sounding tone)

The numbers $\frac{6}{4}$ (usually only 2) placed after a Roman numeral indicate third inversion. The numbers 6, 4, and 2 indicate the letter names (not necessarily the placement) of the fifth, third, and root, respectively.

Example:

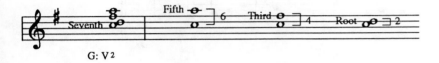

G: V 2

Exercise 7

Identify the inversions of the following dominant seventh chords.

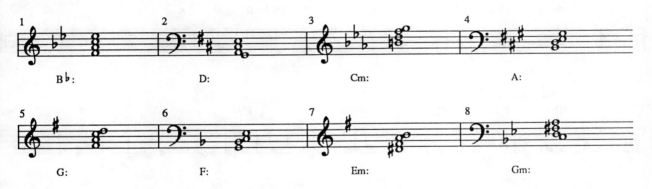

Exercise 8

In the following songs, identify every chord by its tonal relationship (Roman numerals). Give the correct inversion of each as indicated by the chord symbols. Remember, when using chord symbols, the inversions are expressed by two letters (for example, C/ G). The first letter names the chord, while the second identifies the inversion.

Example:

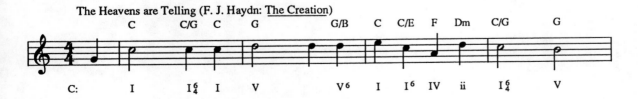

The Heavens are Telling (F. J. Haydn: The Creation)

Exercise 9

In the following songs the chords are written with Roman numerals. Substitute a chord symbol for every Roman numeral. Example:

Waltzing Matilda (J. Barr)

I (D)   IV (G)   I (D)   V⁷ (A⁷)   I (D)

V⁷ (A⁷)   I (D)   IV (G)   I (D)   V⁷ (A⁷)   I (D)

Beautiful Dreamer (S. Foster)

I   IV   V   I

I   IV   V   I

Silent Night (F. Gruber)

I   V⁷   I   IV   I

IV   I   V⁷   I   V⁷   I

Edelweiss (R. Rodgers: The Sound of Music)

I   V⁶₅   I⁶   IV⁶   I⁶₄   vi   ii   V⁷   I

V⁶₅   I⁶   IV⁶   I⁶₄   V⁷   I

Additional Exercises

Sight Singing Exercises

Exercise 1

Sing the following triads and their inversions.

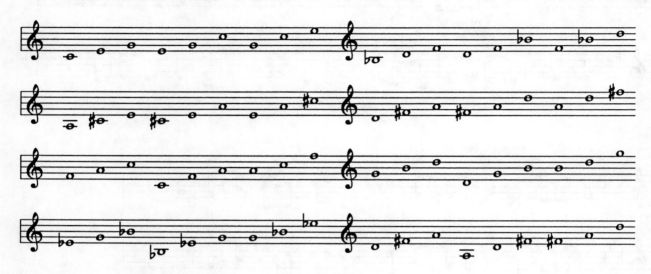

Keyboard Exercises

Exercise 1

Play each of the following sets of chord inversions.

Exercise 2

Play each of the following sets of primary chords in inversions.

Exercise 3

The following pieces use the primary chords in inversions. *Instructor:* Ask a member of the class to play the chords while the rest of the class sings the melody.

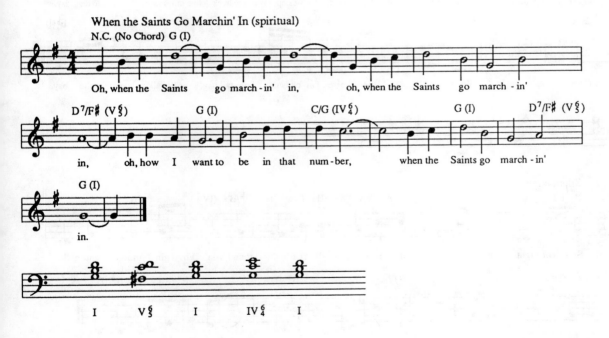

Over the River and Through the Woods (traditional)

O-ver the river and through the woods to grand-mo-ther's house we go, the horse knows the way to car-ry the sleigh through the white and drif-ted snow. O-ver the ri-ver and through the woods, oh, how the wind does blow! It stings the toes and bites the nose as o-ver the ground we go.

Chords:

I — IV$^6_4$ — I — V$^6_5$ — I
D — G/D — D — A^7/C♯ — D

Camptown Races (S. Foster)

The Camp-town lad-ies sing this song, doo da, doo da; the camp-town race track five miles long, oh, doo da day. Goin' to run all night goin' to run all day; the horse I fan-cy is the bob-tail nag, he'll walk a-way from the bay.

Chords:

Silent Night (F. Gruber)

Si - lent night, ho - ly night, all is calm, all is bright, round yon vir - gin mo-ther and child, Ho - ly in-fant so ten-der and mild, sleep in hea-ven-ly peace sleep in hea-ven-ly peace.

Chords:

I — V$^6_5$ — I — IV$^6_4$ — I
B♭ — F^7/A — B♭ — E♭/B♭ — B♭

Chapter 11

Home on the Range (D. Kelley and B. Higley)

Oh, give me a home where the buf-fa-lo roam, where the deer, and the an-te-lope play; where sel-dom is heard a dis-

cour-ag-ing word and the skies are not clou-dy all day. Home, home on the range, where the deer and the an-te-lope

play: where sel-dom is heard a dis - cour-ag-ing word and the skies are not clou-dy all day.

Chords:

I	IV$^6_4$	I	V$^6_5$	I
F	B♭/F	F	C^7/E	F

Other Concepts and Exercises

Writing Triads in Inversions

To write a triad in an inversion use the following steps:

1. Write the triad in its simplest form. For example:

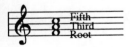

2. Make the third or the fifth the lowest sounding tone depending on the position (inversion) desired.

First Inversion (Third as Lowest Sounding Tone)

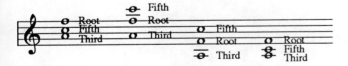

Second Inversion (Fifth as Lowest Sounding Tone)

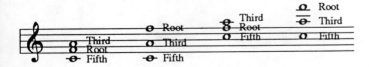

If a chord is to be in root position, no adjustment is necessary.

Exercise 1

Write the following chords in the given inversions. It is possible, of course, to make many different arrangements of inverted chords. For this exercise use only those described in the following section. Example: If a triad is in first inversion, put the root of the chord on top.

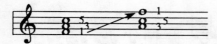

If a triad is in second inversion, put the fifth of the chord on the bottom.

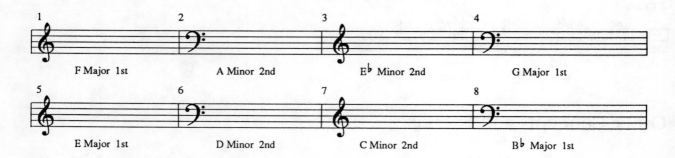

1. F Major 1st
2. A Minor 2nd
3. E♭ Minor 2nd
4. G Major 1st
5. E Major 1st
6. D Minor 2nd
7. C Minor 2nd
8. B♭ Major 1st

Exercise 2

In the following songs write only the chords that are *circled*. Identify each circled chord by using a Roman numeral. Also identify inversions.
Example:

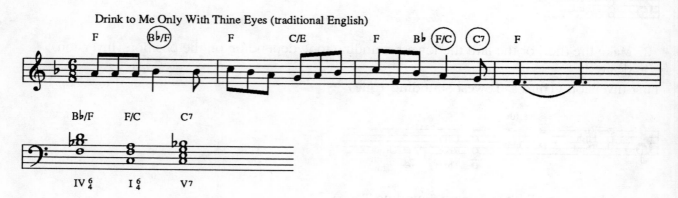

Impossible Dream (M. Leigh: <u>Man of La Mancha</u>)

Edelweiss (R. Rodgers: <u>The Sound of Music</u>)

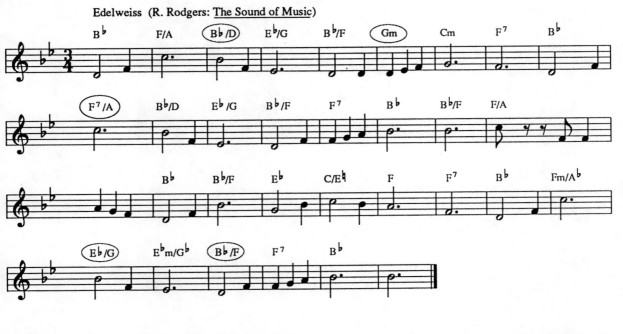

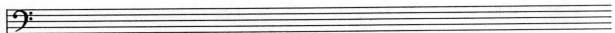

Chapter 12 Melody and Musical Structure

In the previous eleven chapters we have learned to read pitches in the treble and bass clefs as well as rhythms in simple and compound meters. We have also gained some understanding of the major-minor tonal system: scales (keys), intervals, and chords. We have accomplished (to some extent) what we originally set out to do: we have learned to "read" this nonverbal language called music.

Now let's examine musical compositions from another perspective—in terms of **melody** and **melodic structure.** In comparing music to language, we could say that we have learned the words, their definitions, and the parts of speech (nouns, verbs, and so on) and are now ready to put this information to use in learning "sentence" structure.

Melody

We often think of melody as the **pitches** in a song. In a fuller sense, melody is a **marriage** of rhythm, meter, and pitch. Although we may still feel that the pitches are the most important element of a melody, without rhythm and meter these pitches are merely a series of notes.

Example: *Instructor:* Play the following four examples below.

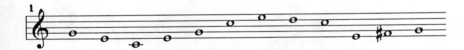

Given the following rhythm and meter, these pitches will now make the melody the "Star Spangled Banner."

Observe how the melody changes if we change the *rhythm.*

Now let's keep the original pitches and rhythm but change the *meter.*

Oh ___ say can you see ___ by the dawn's ear - ly light

Exercise 1

The pitches of the following songs are familiar, but the rhythm and meter have been changed. *Instructors:* Play and sing the following melodies. For *Class Discussion:* Are these new melodies as easy to remember as the original ones? Do you like these new melodies as well?

Old Folks at Home (S. Foster)

Way down up - on the Swa - nee Ri - ver, far, far a - way;

America (traditional)

My coun - try, 'tis of thee, sweet land of li - ber - ty, of thee I sing.

Joy to the World (G. F. Handel)

Joy to the world, the Lord is come; let Earth re - ceive her King!

These illustrations should demonstrate the importance of rhythm and meter in melodies.

What Makes a Good Melody?

The answer is simple: The *right combination* of rhythm, meter, and pitch. Finding the right combination, however, is one of the wonderful mysteries of music. If everyone knew the secret, every piece would have a great melody.

Finding the right combination is also very subjective. Some may consider a particular melody beautiful while others consider the same melody mediocre.

Exercise 2

Instructor: Play the following melodies.
Students: Which melody do you like the best? Which melody is the easiest to remember? Are the answers to these two questions the same?

Nocturne in D♭ (Op. 27, No. 2) (F. Chopin)

Was Ist Sylvia? (F. Schubert)

In der Frühe (H. Wolf)

Due to our present level of musical understanding let's limit our discussion in this chapter to melodies that are (1) easy to sing and (2) easy to remember.

Easy-to-Sing Melodies

1. Melodies that are easy to sing generally are **limited in range** (their range is usually not greater than a tenth, or an octave plus two notes). (See the section on compound intervals in chapter 9.)

    Some people find the "Star Spangled Banner" difficult to sing because of its range of a twelfth (an octave plus four notes).

2. Simple melodies should contain few **leaps.** Most of the movement should be **scalar** (stepwise).

    Instructor: Play the following examples on the piano; then ask students to sing each one.

    Scalar with a few leaps: Not scalar—large leaps:

Easy-to-Remember Melodies

What makes a melody easy to remember? We can remember some melodies after hearing them only once or twice, while others take constant repetition. If you remember a melody quickly it probably has one or more of the following characteristics of rhythm or pitch.

Rhythm

1. Easy-to-remember melodies usually have a limited number of rhythmic patterns.
    Example:

The entire song is composed of only three rhythmic patterns:

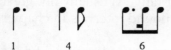

(Take a moment to review the pieces in chapters 3 and 8, observing the rhythmic patterns used in each example.)
Example:

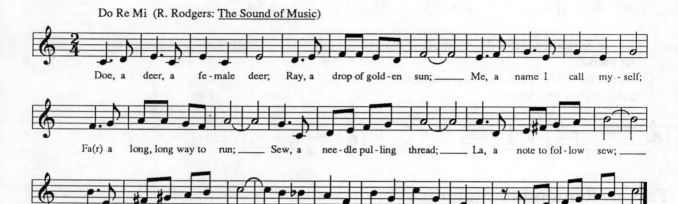

Do Re Mi (R. Rodgers: The Sound of Music)

Doe, a   deer, a   fe-male deer; Ray, a   drop of gold-en sun; ___ Me, a   name I   call   my-self;

Fa(r) a   long, long way to   run; ___ Sew, a   nee-dle pul-ling   thread; ___ La, a   note to fol-low   sew; ___

Tea, a   drink with jam and   bread; ___ that will bring us   back to   doe-oh - oh-oh   Do Re Mi Fa Sol La Ti   Do!

This song is composed of only two rhythmic patterns plus a note twice the length of the pulse note.

Observation: The more rhythmic patterns, the more difficult the rhythm is to remember.
2. Easy-to-remember melodies usually contain a repeating rhythm.
Example: Greensleeves (see previous example)
Measures 1, 2, 3, 5, 6, 10, 11, and 14 all have the same rhythm:

Example: Do Re Mi (see previous example)
Measures 1–4 and 9–12 contain the same rhythm:

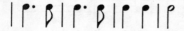

Measures 5–8, 13–16, 17–20, and 21–24 also contain the same rhythm:

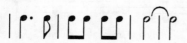

Observation: A piece with little rhythmic repetition would be very difficult to remember after only one or two hearings.

3. Easy-to-remember melodies of songs contain a rhythm that follows the *natural stress* of the WORDS.

   Example: America

   Easy to remember

More difficult to remember

Exercise 3

Analyze the following songs. Identify every rhythmic pattern used in each song. Circle the measures with repeating rhythm. Does the composer follow the natural stress of the text?

Pitch

1. The pitches of an easy-to-remember melody are usually scalar (stepwise): they follow the ascending and descending steps of a scale (major or minor).
   Example:

Joy to the World

2. Melodic leaps are usually small (the interval of a third or fourth) and follow a basic chord outline.
   Example:

Row, Row, Row your Boat

   Example:

The Star Spangled Banner

3. Easy-to-remember melodies make use of melodic repetition.
   Melodic repetition is an *exact* restatement of *both* pitch and rhythm.
   Example:

Greensleeves (traditional)

Melodic repetition occurs in measures 1–2 and 5–6, measures 9–10 and 13–14, measures 7–8, and 15–16, and measures 3 and 11.

4. Easy-to-remember melodies make use of **sequence.**

Sequence is a restatement (of both pitch and rhythm) on a *different pitch.*

The song "Do Re Mi" is based on three ideas (**motives**). Each idea is restated on a different pitch (sequence). In the following example, a letter in brackets identifies the original melodic idea (motive). A letter followed by a number identifies the corresponding sequence.

Example:

Do Re Mi (R. Rodgers: <u>The Sound of Music</u>)

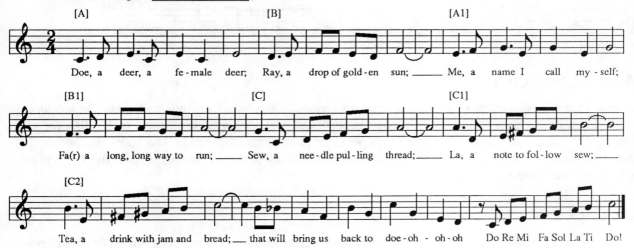

Exercise 4

Analyze the following songs. Bracket the scalar passages, and chord outlines. Also bracket and identify examples of melodic repetition and sequence. (See the previous examples.)

Impossible Dream (M. Leigh: Man of La Mancha)

Musical Structure

Writing a melody is similar to writing several sentences in English. In English we write dependent and independent clauses. In music we write antecedent and consequent phrases. In English we use a comma (,) to separate dependent from independent clauses and a period (.) to show the end of a *complete* sentence (idea). In music we use a **cadence** (half or authentic), instead of the comma or period, to signal the end of a phrase.

Cadences

A cadence is a point of arrival (resting point). It may be a *momentary* point of arrival or a *final* one. This resting point is often made melodically by a note of long duration.
Example:

Do Re Mi (R. Rodgers: The Sound of Music)

Doe, a deer, a fe-male deer; Ray, a drop of gold-en sun; ___

The resting point may also be marked by a rest at the end of the phrase.
Example:

Greensleeves (traditional)

I have loved ___ you for so long, ___ De - light - ing in ___ your com - pa - ny.

There are four main types of cadences: half, authentic, deceptive, and plagal. For the moment let's concentrate on the first two: half and authentic. (Deceptive and plagal cadences will be discussed later in the chapter.)

Half Cadences

A half cadence is an arrival on the dominant (the chord built on the fifth scale step).
Example:

Edelweiss (R. Rodgers: The Sound Of Music)

F7

The half cadence is similar to a dependent clause. It leaves you with a desire to hear more.
(Remember that the dominant chord has a strong "pull" to the tonic triad.)

Authentic Cadences

An authentic cadence is an arrival on the tonic triad *preceded* by the dominant chord.
Example:

Edelweiss

F7   Bb

The authentic cadence is similar to an independent clause. It leaves you with a feeling of
completion.

Antecedent and Consequent Phrases

When a musical phrase ending with a half cadence is followed by a phrase ending with an authentic
cadence, we speak of the phrases being **antecedent** and **consequent,** respectively. An antecedent
and consequent phrase make a musical **period** (complete idea).
Example:

Edelweiss
Antecedent

F7

Half Cadence

Consequent

F7   Bb

Authentic Cadence

Exercise 5

Instructor: Play the following songs.
Students: Sing the songs. Find the point of arrival of each phrase. Identify the cadence by the last chord(s) in the phrase. Bracket the antecedent and consequent phrases. (See the previous example.)

Old Folks at Home (S. Foster)

Lullaby (Wiegenlied) (J. Brahms)

(In this example the rest is *not* an indication of the end of a phrase.)

Exercise 6

Make a complete analysis of the following melodies (key, meter, rhythm, pitch, and cadences).
Example:

Greensleeves (traditional)

A - las my love___ you do me wrong,___ To cast me off___ dis - courte - ous - ly; And

I have loved___ you for so long,___ De - light - ing in___ your com - pa - ny.

Green - sleeves___ was all my joy,___ Green - sleeves___ was my de - light,

Green - sleeves was my heart of gold,___ And who but my la - dy Green - sleeves.

Analysis

Key: E Minor

Meter: Duple Compound (two beats per measure, dotted quarter note is the pulse note)

Rhythm:

1. Uses only three rhythmic patterns:

2. Rhythmic repetition:

    Measures 1, 2, 3, 5, 6, 10, 11, 14

    Measures 4, 8

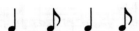

    Measures 7, 15

    Measures 9, 13

Pitch:

1. The melody is a mixture of stepwise movement and small leaps.
2. Measure 5 contains a perfect fifth followed by a perfect fourth.
3. There are two examples of large leaps: measures 8–9 (E up to D: a minor seventh) and measures 12–13 (B up to D: a minor tenth. See chapter 9).
4. Melodic repetition:
    Measures 1–2 are repeated in measures 5–6.
    Measures 9–10 are repeated in measures 13–14.
    Measures 7–8 are repeated in measures 15–16.
    Measure 3 is repeated in measure 11.
5. Sequences: No examples.

Cadences:

1. Half: measure 4 (antecedent phrase)
2. Authentic: measure 8 (consequent phrase)
3. Half: measure 12 (antecedent phrase II)
4. Authentic: measure 16 (consequent phrase II)

In this example there are *two* periods (measures 1–8 and 9–16). Each period is a **parallel period.** A "parallel period" has a consequent phrase that *begins* exactly like the antecedent phrase.

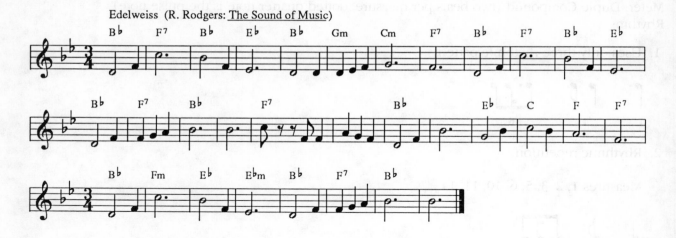

Other Cadences

Deceptive Cadences

A deceptive cadence is a resolution to an unexpected chord. We normally expect the dominant chord to resolve to the tonic triad. It may, however, resolve to the submediant triad (a chord built on the sixth scale step), which shares two tones with the tonic.
Example:

Example:

Other types of deceptive cadences are also possible, but this is the most common.

Plagal Cadences

A plagal cadence (sometimes referred to as the "Amen" cadence because of its traditional use at the end of hymns) is an arrival on the tonic triad *preceded* by the subdominant triad (a chord built on the fourth scale step).
Example:

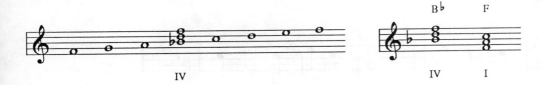

Example:

Exercise 7

Make some analyses of melodies you like. Do they have characteristics in common?

Additional Exercises

Sight Singing Exercises

Exercise 1

Sing the following melodies.

Keyboard Exercises

Exercise 1

Play the following chord progressions using the three primary chords (I, IV, and V).

I   IV $^6_4$ I   V $^6_5$ I

I   V $^6_5$ I   IV   V $^6_5$ I

I   V $^6_4$ I^6 IV   V^2 I^6 IV   I

Exercise 2

Harmonize each of the following melodies using only the primary chords. Trial and error at this stage is important; decide by ear where the chord changes occur. *Experiment.* There may be more than one solution.

Some helpful hints for harmonizing simple songs include:

1. Tones with the longest duration are usually chord tones.
2. Chord changes *usually* occur on strong beats.
3. Not every tone of the melody needs to fit in the chord that sounds at that time.
4. The dominant triad resolves to the tonic triad (when using only primary chords).
5. Look for chord outlines in the melody.

Example:

Frere Jacques (French folksong)

Possible Harmonizations:

Jingle Bells (J. Pierpont)

Jin - gle bells,   jin - gle bells,   jin - gle all the   way;   oh, what fun   it   is to ride in a   one horse o - pen   sleigh.

G (I)   C/G (IV⁶₄)   D⁷/F♯ (V⁶₅)

Twinkle, Twinkle Little Star (N. Dezede)

Twin-kle, twin-kle, lit-tle star, how I won-der where you are, up a-bove the world so high, like a dia-mond in the sky, twin-kle, twin-kle, lit-tle star, how I won-der where you are.

D (I)   G/D (IV$^6_4$)   A^7/C♯ (V$^6_5$)

Yankee Doodle (traditional)

Yan-kee Doo-dle went to town a- rid-ing on a po-ny, he stuck a fea-ther in his cap and called it ma-ca-ro-ni. Yan-kee Doo-dle, keep it up, Yan-kee Doo-dle Dan-dy, mind the mus-ic and the step, and with the girls be han-dy.

B♭(I)   E♭/B♭(IV$^6_4$)   F^7/A (V$^6_5$)

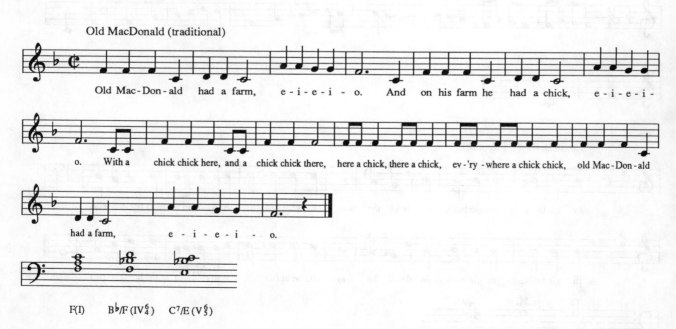

Old MacDonald (traditional)

Old Mac-Don-ald had a farm, e-i-e-i-o. And on his farm he had a chick, e-i-e-i-o. With a chick chick here, and a chick chick there, here a chick, there a chick, ev-'ry-where a chick chick, old Mac-Don-ald had a farm, e-i-e-i-o.

F(I)   B♭/F (IV$^6_4$)   C^7/E (V$^6_5$)

Exercise 3

Variations on piano accompaniments. Play the songs in exercise 2 using one or more of the accompaniment figures below.
Examples:

Chapter 13 *Musical Form*

In chapter 12 we discovered that the song "Greensleeves" is composed of two parallel periods. Example:

The **form** of this piece is identified (classified) as a *two-part song form.* The song is divided into two symmetrically balanced sections, each concluding with a strong (and in this case, authentic) cadence.

Songs may be written in many different forms. We will limit our discussion to the two most frequently used.

Two-Part Song Form (Binary Form)

In analyzing the form of a piece, a **part** may be a single phrase, a period, or even two periods in length. The *basic* design of the two-part song form, however, is generally two periods: A A ‖ B B or simply A B.

Example:

In this example, the first *part* (A) is a parallel period since both the antecedent and consequent phrases begin in the same manner. The second *part* (B) is a contrasting period, because the consequent phrase is musically different from the antecedent phrase.

In the song "Wiegenlied" (Cradle-Song) by Johannes Brahms, the first part (A) is a contrasting period since the consequent phrase is musically different from the antecedent phrase. The second part (B) is a parallel period because both the antecedent and consequent phrases begin in the same manner.

Example:

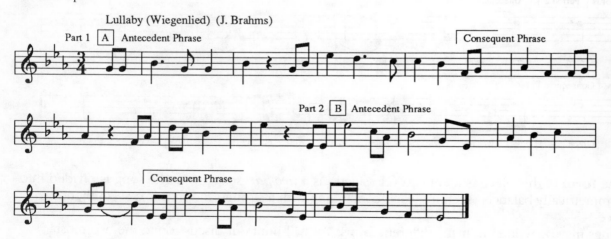

Exercise 1

The following songs can be classified as two-part song form.
Instructor: Play each song.
Students:

1. Decide the end of each phrase.
2. Bracket the periods and identify each as either parallel or contrasting.

Yankee Doodle (traditional)

Londonderry Air (Irish Folksong)

Three-Part Song Form (Ternary Form)

The major characteristic of the three-part (incipient) song form is a return of the "A" section. The musical shape is expressed as A B A: theme (A), contrasting theme (B), return of the theme (A). Example:

Twinkle, Twinkle, Little Star

In most examples of three-part form, the first part (A) is *usually repeated,* making a parallel period (A A). The second part consists of a contrasting phrase (B). The third part is a repetition of the initial *phrase* (A) that cadences on the tonic of the key. The form is therefore A A ‖ B A ‖.

Example:

Edelweiss begins with a parallel period (measures 1–16): A A. Measures 17–24 consist of a contrasting phrase: B. The final phrase is a return to the A theme (phrase), an exact repetition of the consequent phrase of the first period (compare measures 25–32 and measures 9–16).

What may appear at first glance to be two periods (and therefore a two-part (binary) form is actually a three-part form due to the return of A. Because of this similar look, the three-part song form is sometimes referred to as a **rounded binary form.**

In popular music we sometimes speak of the contrasting section (B) as the bridge. (The letter B does *not* stand for bridge but for a contrasting phrase.)

We have seen that a **part** can be larger than a **phrase.** In the song "On the Street Where You Live" each part is a **period** in length. The melody for the first, second, and fourth periods are the same. The third period is contrasting material (the bridge). The song, therefore, is in a **three-part form:**

A A B A [Part I is A repeated (A A), Part II is B, and Part III is the return of A.]

Example:

Exercise 2

The following songs can be classified as three-part (incipient) song form.

Instructor: Play each song.

Students:

1. Identify the end of each phrase.
2. *Bracket* phrases with the same melody and identify each with the capital letter A.
3. Finally, identify the contrasting theme with the capital letter B.

Deck the Halls (traditional)

Somewhere Over the Rainbow (H. Arlen: The Wizard of Oz)

When writing a song, composers first conceive a musical idea. They may *repeat* the idea exactly or with some *variation*. They may also invent another musical idea as a *contrast* to the first. When we analyze the form of a song, we are basically finding the order (arrangement) of these musical ideas (including their repetitions, variations, and contrasting themes).

We have seen that the two-part and three-part song forms each contain two contrasting musical ideas (A and B). It is the order and arrangement of these ideas that make the specific song form.

Exercise 3

Identify the form of each of the following pieces using the following steps.
Instructor: Play each song.
Students:

1. Identify the end of each phrase.
2. Label each of the phrases with capital letters (A, B). (Phrases with the same *basic* melody should be identified by the same letter.)
3. Identify the form: two-part song form or three-part (rounded binary) song form.
   Example:

Ode to Joy (L. van Beethoven)

This example is in three-part form: A A ‖ B A ‖

Drink to Me Only with Thine Eyes (traditional)

Old Folks at Home (S. Foster)

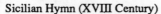

Sicilian Hymn (XVIII Century)

Camptown Races (S. Foster)

'Tis the Last Rose of Summer (Irish Air)

Repeating Sections of Music

In each of the musical examples in this chapter, entire sections of music have been repeated. A variety of words and symbols have been created to save the composer time writing repeated sections of music.

The Repeat Sign

The repeat sign is used whenever a section is to be repeated *exactly*.

$\|: \quad :\|$

The repeat sign consists of a double bar with two dots placed at the beginning of a section to be repeated, and then another double bar with two dots placed at the end.
Example:

Impossible Dream (M. Leigh: <u>Man of La Mancha</u>)

When signaling a repeat back to the beginning of a piece, only the second half of the repeat sign is necessary. (This is because there is no bar line after the key signature.)
Example:

Now Thank We All Our God (J. Crüger)

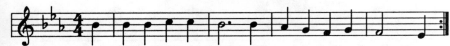

Multiple Endings

Multiple endings are used when the *beginning* of a section is to be repeated but the ending is different the second (or third or fourth) time.

In this example, the *beginning* of the piece (measures 1–6) is played three times. The last two bars of this eight-bar phrase differ on each repeat. The first time, you would play bars 1–8; the second time, bars 1–6, then bars 9–10; and the third time, bars 1–6, then bars 11–12.

D.C. al Fine (Da Capo al Fine)

Da capo (from the head) *al fine* (to the end) is used when you want to repeat only a portion of the beginning of a piece (not the entire section).

In this example, the entire section (measures 1–12) is played first; then measures 1–6 are repeated.

D.S. al Fine (Dal Segno al Fine)

Dal segno (from the sign, 𝄋) *al fine* (to the end) is used when you want to repeat a section within the piece.

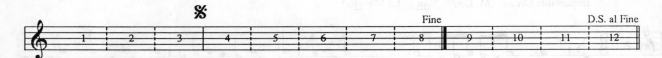

In this example, the entire section (measures 1–12) is played first; then measures 4–8 are played.

Coda

A *coda* (from the Italian meaning *tail, end*) is a closing section added to create a feeling of finality. The actual coda is always placed at the end of a piece; however, directions for getting to the coda may vary.

Multiple Endings to Coda

Performed: 1–8, 1–6, 9–10, 1–6, 11–13, 1–3, 14–16

D.C. al Coda: Da Capo al Coda (From the Beginning to the Coda)

When you come to the words *D.C. al Coda,* go back to the beginning of the piece and play until you reach the words *To Coda* ⊕. Then skip to the coda (the section at the end of the piece).

Performed: 1–12, 1–7, 13–15

D.S. al Coda: Dal Segno al Coda (From the Sign to the Coda)

When you come to the words *D.S. al Coda,* go back to the sign 𝄋 and play until you reach the words *To Coda* ⊕. Then skip to the coda (section at the end of the piece).

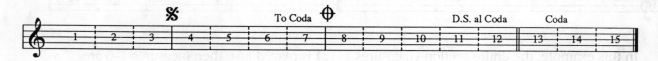

Performed: 1–12, 4–7, 13–15

Exercise 4

Discuss the following pieces. Decide which sections are to be repeated. Use the measure numbers to make your explanations clear. (An anacrusis is *not* counted as the first measure. The first measure of any piece is always the first *complete* measure.)
Example:

Performed: A 1 2 3 4 5 6 7 8 (A) 1 2 3 4 5 6 7 8 9 10 11 12 5 6 7 8

We Wish You A Merry Christmas (English Folksong)

Chapter 13

Chapter 14 *Review*

In the past thirteen chapters we have discussed the various aspects of music that are essential to reading and understanding this nonverbal language. We have learned that music shares characteristics of both language and mathematics.

The chapters in this text are arranged to provide some variety in learning the Fundamentals of Music. It would have been possible, for example, to discuss all of the aspects of pitch (reading notes, accidentals, scales, intervals) before discussing rhythm. Now let's put these individual chapters into perspective by reviewing the major elements of music fundamentals with respect to (1) pitch, (2) rhythm-meter, and (3) harmony.

Use this chapter as a quick reference and for practice. After reviewing this section, make a complete musical analysis of the pieces beginning on page 243.

Pitch

The Grand Staff and the Keyboard

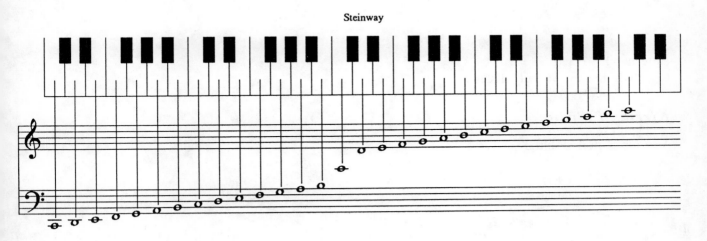

Accidentals

A *sharp* raises a pitch by a half-step.

A *flat* lowers a pitch by a half-step.

A *natural* sign cancels a sharp or flat.

Enharmonic tones have the same sound and different spellings.

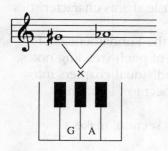

Major Scales

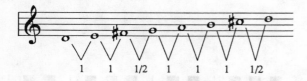

Pattern 1 1 ½ 1 1 1 ½
(1 = whole step, ½ = half-step)

Circle of Fifths

A series of perfect fifths.

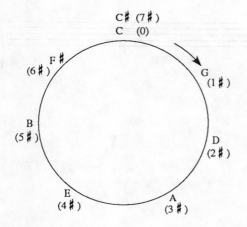

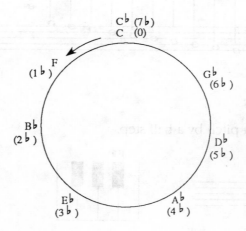

Placement of Accidentals in a Key Signature

FCGDAEB

BEADGCF

Relative Minor Scales

Relative minor scales share key signatures with major scales located a minor third above.

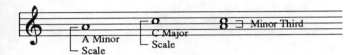

A Minor Scale · C Major Scale · Minor Third

Three Forms of the Minor Scale

1. Natural (pure): No adjustments.

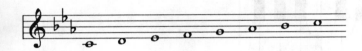

2. Harmonic: Raised seventh in the scale (or piece). The key signature remains unchanged.

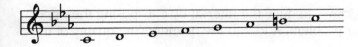

3. Melodic: Raised sixth and seventh ascending, lowered sixth and seventh descending in the scale (or piece). The key signature remains unchanged.

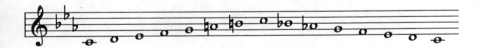

Intervals

From the tonic to scale steps 2, 3, 6, and 7 is a *major* distance. From the tonic to scale steps 1, 4, 5, and 8 is a *perfect* distance.

Steps in Computing Intervals

1. Count (to identify the quantity).
2. Apply the key signature of the bottom note (to identify major and perfect intervals).
3. Compare (when identifying intervals) or adjust (when writing intervals) according to the formula:

diminished ◄— minor ◄— **Major** —► Augmented

2, 3, 6, 7

diminished ◄— **Perfect** —► Augmented

1, 4, 5, 8

(Each arrow represents a half-step adjustment.)

Tri-tone

Augmented Fourth or Diminished Fifth   Three Whole Steps (six half-steps)

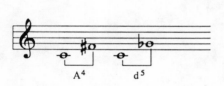

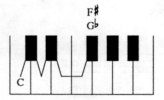

Compound Intervals

Compound intervals are intervals larger than an octave. Reduce the interval by transposing the upper note down an octave; then compute it as a regular problem. Add 7 to the quantity (the quality of the interval is unchanged).

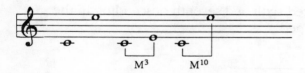

Melody

A melody is a union of pitch and rhythm (meter).

Cadences

A cadence is a point of arrival (resting point).

Half cadence: An arrival on the dominant (chord built on the fifth scale step).

Authentic cadence: An arrival on the tonic (chord built on the first scale step), *preceded by the dominant.*

Deceptive cadence: Usually a dominant resolving to a submediant triad (chord built on the sixth scale step).

Plagal: An arrival on the tonic, *preceded by the subdominant* (chord built on the fourth scale step). Sometimes referred to as the "Amen" cadence.

Rhythm-Meter

Rhythm: The length of a sound.

Types of Notes (representing sound)   **Rests** (representing silence)

o	Whole		▬	Whole
♩	Half		▬	Half
♩	Quarter		𝄽	Quarter
♪	Eighth		𝄾	Eighth
♬	Sixteenth		𝄿	Sixteenth

Relative Values of Notes

o = 1   o = 2   o = 4   o = 8

♩ = 1/2   ♩ = 1   ♩ = 2   ♩ = 4

♩ = 1/4   ♩ = 1/2   ♩ = 1   ♩ = 2

♪ = 1/8   ♪ = 1/4   ♪ = 1/2   ♪ = 1

Dot

A dot placed *after* a note increases the value of that note by half.

If ♩ = 2 beats, then ♩• = 3 beats.

If ♩ = 1 beat, then ♩• = 1 1/2 beats.

Ties

Notes may be tied together (⌒) to form one sound that cannot be expressed by a single note or to connect notes from one measure to another.

$\frac{4}{4}$ ♩ ♬ = 2 1/4 Beats $\frac{4}{4}$ o ♩ = 6 Beats

Fermata

⌢ A fermata symbol is used to stop the beat that is measuring the length of sound.

Beat: A constant pulse

Meter: The grouping of the beat

    Duple: A grouping of *two* beats

    Triple: A grouping of *three* beats

    Quadruple: A grouping of *four* beats

Pulse Note: The note chosen to represent the beat

Simple and Compound Meters

Simple meters are meters in which the pulse note is divisible into *two* even notes.

Compound meters are meters in which the pulse note is divisible into *three* even notes. Compound meters have dotted notes as pulse notes.

Time Signatures

Time signatures are expressed as two numbers, one above the other.

$$\frac{4}{4} \quad \frac{6}{8}$$

In simple meters, the top number is 2, 3, or 4. It represents the meter (grouping).

In compound meters, the top number is 6, 9, or 12. These numbers are *three times larger* than their respective meters.

In simple meters, the bottom number is 1, 2, 4, 8, or 16. It represents the pulse note. *The quarter note* (represented by the number 4) *is the most frequently used pulse note.*

In compound meters, the bottom number is 2, 4, 8, or 16. It represents the *division* of the pulse note. *The dotted quarter note is the most frequently used pulse note* in compound meters. The bottom number used in the meter sign when the pulse note is a dotted quarter note is 8. (Three eighth notes make a dotted quarter note.)

Other Time Signatures

C Usually referred to as "common time"; equal to $\frac{4}{4}$ meter

¢ Usually referred to as "cut time"; equal to $\frac{2}{2}$ meter

Beaming

In both simple and compound meters, notes are beamed if

1. They have flags.

Simple Meter   **Compound Meter**

2. They are equal to the pulse note (showing the beginning and ending of a beat). Notes of different values may be beamed together.

Simple Meter   **Compound Meter**

   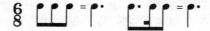

3. They form a division of the pulse note.

Simple Meter   **Compound Meter**

Anacrusis: One or several notes that occur before the first (strong) beat. The anacrusis can be used in either simple or compound meters.

Anacrusis

Triplet: A compound division in a simple meter.

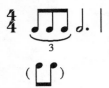

Three = two of the same type of note

Harmony

Chord: Three or more notes sounding together.

Four Types of Triads

Major	Minor	Diminished	Augmented
1, 3, 5 of the major scale	Lower the third of a major triad	Lower the third and fifth of a major triad	Raise the fifth of a major triad

Intervallic Relationship of Triads

Major   Minor   Diminished   Augmented

Chord Symbols

Symbol	Chord Identification
D	D major triad
Dm	D minor triad
D°, D dim.	D diminished triad
D⁺, D Aug.	D augmented triad
D7	D major triad with an added minor seventh above the root. (This seventh creates a *tri-tone* with the third.)

Relationship of Chords in a Key

Major Mode:

I   ii   iii   IV   V   vi   vii°

Harmonic Minor Mode:

i   ii°   III⁺   iv   V   VI   vii°

Chord Inversions

$^6_3$ **First Inversion** (The third of the chord is the lowest sounding tone.)

$^6_4$ **Second Inversion** (The fifth of the chord is the lowest sounding tone.)

V⁷ **Dominant Seventh Chord (Root Position)**
V$^6_5$ **Dominant Seventh Chord (First Inversion)** (The third of the chord is the lowest sounding tone.)
V$^4_3$ **Dominant Seventh Chord (Second Inversion)** (The fifth of the chord is the lowest sounding tone.)
V² **Dominant Seventh Chord (Third Inversion)** (The seventh of the chord is the lowest sounding tone.)

Additional Concepts

Duplet: A simple division in a compound meter.

Two = three of the same type of note

Double Accidentals
× Double sharp: Raises a pitch one whole step
♭♭ Double flat: Lowers a pitch one whole step

Analysis

Make a complete musical analysis of the following pieces with regard to pitch, rhythm (meter) and harmony.

Instructor: Discuss the following pieces in class or ask students to choose and analyze one of the pieces.

Pitch

Identify all pitches.
Identify the key signature, decide on tonality: major or minor.
Compute intervals in the melody (pick several measures).
Find the ends of phrases. Identify the cadences.
Find melodic repetition, sequence.

Rhythm-Meter

Identify the meter: simple or compound.
Identify the pulse note.
Sing the rhythm (use syllables). Think in *patterns*.
Identify the values of rests and ties.
Does the piece begin with an anacrusis? Does it contain a fermata?
Does the piece contain triplets?

Harmony

Explain all chord symbols.
Write every chord in the piece.

My Object All Sublime (Gilbert and Sullivan: <u>The Mikado</u>)

Deck the Halls (traditional)

Black Is the Color (traditional)

Black, black, black is the co-lor of my true love's hair, her lips are won-drous ro-sy fair, and the pret-ti-est face and the dain-ti-est hands; I love the ground where on she stands.

Impossible Dream (M. Leigh: Man of La Mancha)

1.To dream the im-pos-si-ble dream, to fight the un-beat-a-ble foe, to
(2. To) right the un-right-a-ble wrong, to love pure and chase from a-far to

bear with un-bear-a-ble sor-row to run where the brave dare not go 2. To reach the un-reach-a-ble
try when your arms are too wea-ry to

star! This is my quest, to fol-low that star, no mat-ter how hope-less no mat-ter how far to fight for the

right with-out quest-ion or pause, to be will-ing to march in-to hell for a heav-en-ly cause! And I know that I'll al-ways be

true to this glo-ri-ous quest, that my heart will lie peace-ful and calm, when I'm laid to my rest and the

world will be bet-ter for this; that one man, scorned and cov-ered with scars, still strove with his last ounce of

cou-rage to reach the un-reach-a-ble stars.

Appendix 1 Making Music "Musical"

Music is more than playing or singing the right pitches and rhythms. The next three pages will discuss the elements that help make music performance more exciting, more enjoyable . . . more "musical."

Dynamics

Dynamics (force) pertain to the degree of volume (loudness or softness) achieved by pressure or force. Dynamic markings are generally written in abbreviated Italian.

pp	(*pianissimo*):	Very soft
p	(*piano*):	Soft
mp	(*mezzo piano*):	Medium soft (literally: half-soft)
mf	(mezzo forte):	Medium loud (half-loud)
f	(forte):	Loud
ff	(fortissimo):	Very loud

The earliest dynamics were used around 1500 A.D. (No expression marks have been found in music prior to that time.)

Some composers have used extreme dynamic markings: Giuseppe Verdi (nineteenth-century operatic composer) used *ppppp,* while Peter I. Tschaikovsky (nineteenth-century symphonic composer) used *fffff.*

Around 1709, Bartolommeo Cristofori invented a musical instrument called a *pianoforte* or *forte-piano* (known today as a *piano*). This instrument could play soft or loud depending on the amount of pressure (force) exerted by the player.

Other Dynamic Markings

fp	(*forte-piano*):	Loud followed immediately by soft
sfz	(*sforzato,* or *sforzando*):	Forced

Symbols or Words that Change Dynamics

Subito (*SU*-bito): Suddenly, instantly. This term may be used with any dynamic marking to indicate an immediate change—for example, *Subito p* (instantly soft) or *Subito f* (instantly loud).

Crescendo (*cresc.*): Gradually growing louder

Decrescendo (*decres.*): Gradually growing softer

Diminuendo (same as decrescendo)

Expression

Following are a few of the most frequently used terms indicating how a composition should be performed (in terms of mood, atmosphere, or quality).

Dolce (It.): Sweet
Zart (Ger.): Sweet
Ruhig (Ger.): Calm, tranquil
Leggiero (It.): Light
Leicht (Ger.): Light, easy
Pesante (It.): Heavy
Sostenuto (It.): Sustained, supported
Sotto voce (It.): Literally, under the voice, soft

Agitato (It.): Aggitated

Dolorosa (It.): Sad

Accent Marks

Accent marks create a stress on notes that are not normally emphasized (due to meter or rhythm). There are various types of accent marks in use.
Examples:

Accent marks originated in ancient Greek writing, indicating a change of inflection in recitation.

Articulation Marks

Articulation marks are used to indicate clarity and specific rendition in a musical composition. There are many different articulation marks used. The following are the most common.
Legato (It.): Literally, bound, tied-up; to be played smoothly, without interruption.

Legatissimo: Very legato.
Slur: To connect notes of *different* pitch.   (Not to be confused with the tie, which connects notes of the same pitch.)

Staccato (It.): Literally, to separate, to loosen; to be played detached, not connected.

Staccatissimo: Very staccato.
Portate: Midway between legato and staccato.

Portamento (It.): Literally, to carry; in vocal music, a gliding from one tone to another.

Portamento

Appendix 2 Tempo Indications

The time signature does *not* indicate **tempo** (the speed at which a piece is to be performed). There are two ways to indicate tempo.

The Metronome

The metronome is an instrument that produces regular beats at adjustable speeds. Tempo indications are generally expressed in terms of the pulse note. The number refers to beats per minute.

   M.M. ♩ = 60   (60 even beats per minute, or one beat per second)

(M.M. is an abbreviation for *M*aelzel's *M*etronome. The metronome was invented by Dietrich Nikolaus Winkel around 1812, but it is named after Johannes Maelzel, who exploited Winkel's invention. All metronomic markings prior to this time are editorial. (See the music of J. S. Bach, F. J. Haydn, and W. A. Mozart.)

Words

Words may be used to express the speed of a piece; however, in many instances they indicate a mood or feeling and not a speed. (After all, how fast is "fast?") These words are usually Italian, but may also be French or German, and sometimes English.

   Here are a few of the more common tempo markings with their literal meanings. All are Italian terms except where indicated.

Terms Used for Slow Speeds

- *Adagio:* At ease
- *Grave:* Heavy, serious, solemn.
- *Langsam* (Ger.): Slow.
- *Largo:* With breath; very slow.
- *Lent* (Fr.): Slow.
- *Lento:* Slow.

Terms Used for Moderate Speeds

- *Andante:* To go, to walk.
- *Maestoso:* Majestic.
- *Massig* (Ger.): Moderate.
- *Moderato:* Moderate.

Terms Used for Fast Speeds

Allegro: Cheerful, gay, happy.
Allegretto: Rather jolly; somewhat brisk.
Anime (Fr.): Animated; give life to.
Bewegt (Ger.): Move, agitate, excite.
Lebhaft (Ger.): Lively, vivacious, spirited.
Presto: Very fast, swift.
Schnell (Ger.): Rapid, swift.
Vif (Fr.): Alive, living.
Vivace: Brisk, lively.
Vivo: Alive, living.

Terms Used to Change Speed

Accelerando (*Acc.*): Quickening the movement; accelerating.
Allargando (*Allarg.*): Slowing down.
Meno: Less.
Molto: Very much; greatly.
Mosso: Moved, agitated.
Poco: Little.
Piu: More.
Ritardando (*Ritard.*): Becoming slower; gradually slackening.
Ritenuto (*Rit.*): Kept back; immediate reduction of speed.
Stringendo (*String.*): To compress, to tighten (quickening the movement).

Additional Terms and Markings

Appena: Very little.
Assai: Much, very much.
   9   Breath mark.
   //   *Caesura:* Pause or break.
Cantabile: Singing.
Espressivo: Expressive.
Quasi: Almost.
Refrain (*Chorus*): A phrase or verse that recurs at intervals in a song (usually at the end of each stanza).
Tenuto (*Ten.*): Hold.

Tempo Markings

The following are terms used to alter tempos.
A Tempo: Term used after a change of tempo (*ritardando, accelerando*) to indicate a return to the *last tempo before the change.*
Rubato: (It.: Literally, to rob or steal): A deliberately unsteady tempo; stretching and relaxing the tempo.
Tempo I (*Tempo Primo*): Usually used after several tempo changes to indicate a return to the *first (original) tempo of the piece.*

Credits

"Do Re Mi"(from *The Sound of Music*.) Lyrics by Oscar Hammerstein II. Music by Richard Rodgers. Copyright © 1959 by Richard Rodgers and Oscar Hammerstein II. WILLIAMSON MUSIC owner of publication and allied rights throughout the Western Hemisphere and Japan. International Copyright Secured. ALL RIGHTS RESERVED.

"Moon River." Words by Johnny Mercer. Music by Henry Mancini. © 1961 by Famous Music Corp., 1 Gulf and Western Plaza, New York, NY 10023. International Copyright Secured. Made in U.S.A. All Rights Reserved.

"Summertime." Words by DuBose Heyward. Music by George Gershwin. Copyright © 1935 by Gershwin Publishing Corporation. Copyright renewed, assigned to Chappell & Co. International Copyright Secured. ALL RIGHTS RESERVED. Printed in the U.S.A.

"People." Words by Bob Merrill. Music by Jule Styne. Copyright © 1963 & 1964 by Bob Merrill and Jule Styne. Chappell-Styne, Inc. and Wonderful Music Corp., owners of publication and allied rights. International Copyright secured. ALL RIGHTS RESERVED. Printed in the U.S.A.

"My Funny Valentine." Words by Lorenz Hart. Music by Richard Rodgers. Copyright © 1937 by Chappell & Co. Copyright renewed. International Copyright Secured. ALL RIGHTS RESERVED. Printed in the U.S.A.

"Climb Every Mountain" (from *The Sound of Music*.) Lyrics by Oscar Hammerstein II. Music by Richard Rodgers. Copyright © 1959 by Richard Rodgers and Oscar Hammerstein II. Copyright renewed. WILLIAMSON MUSIC owner of publication and allied rights throughout the Western Hemisphere and Japan. International Copyright Secured. ALL RIGHTS RESERVED.

"I Have Dreamed" (from *The King and I*.) Lyrics by Oscar Hammerstein II. Music by Richard Rodgers. Copyright © 1951 by Richard Rodgers and Oscar Hammerstein II. Copyright renewed. WILLIAMSON MUSIC owner of publication and allied rights throughout the Western Hemisphere and Japan. International Copyright Secured. ALL RIGHTS RESERVED.

"The Ballad of John and Yoko." Words and music by John Lennon and Paul McCartney. Copyright © 1969 NORTHERN SONGS LIMITED. All Rights Controlled and Administered by SBK BLACKWOOD MUSIC INC. under license from ATV MUSIC (MACLEN). All Rights Reserved. International Copyright Secured.

"On the Street Where You Live" (from *My Fair Lady*.) Words by Alan Jay Lerner. Music by Frederick Loewe. Copyright © 1956 by Alan Jay Lerner and Frederick Loewe. Chappell & Co. owner of publication and allied rights throughout the world. International Copyright Secured. ALL RIGHTS RESERVED. Printed in the U.S.A.

"Joy to the World" by Hoyt Axton. Published by Lady Jane Music, Hollywood, California.

"I Want to Hold Your Hand." Words and music by John Lennon and Paul McCartney. © Copyright 1963, by Northern Songs Ltd. London, England. Sole Selling Agent Music Corporation of America, Inc. New York, NY. International Copyright Secured. Made in the U.S.A. All Rights Reserved.

"Sabbath Prayer" (from the Musical *Fiddler on the Roof*.) Words by Sheldon Harnick. Music by Jerry Bock. Copyright © 1964 by Alley Music Corporation and Trio Music Company, Inc. All rights administered by Hudson Bay Music, Inc. International Copyright Secured. Made in U.S.A. All Rights Reserved. Used by permission.

"Around the World." Words and Music by Victor Young and Harold Adamson. Copyright © 1956 by Victor Young Publications, Inc. Copyright Renewed, Assigned to Chappell & Co., and Liza Music Corp. International Copyright Secured. ALL RIGHTS RESERVED. Printed in the U.S.A.

"Yellow Submarine." Words and Music by John Lennon and Paul McCartney. Copyright © 1966 NORTHERN SONGS LIMITED. All Rights Controlled and Administered by SBK BLACKWOOD MUSIC INC., under license from ATV MUSIC (MACLEN). All Rights Reserved. International Copyright Secured.

"Mack the Knife" (from *The ThreePenny Opera*.) by Kurt Weill. Copyright © European American Music.

Index of Musical Examples

Index of Musical Examples

Subject Index